WORD PROCESSING

WORD PROCESSING

FIRST STEP TO
THE OFFICE OF
THE FUTURE?

Kathleen Foley Curley

PRAEGER SPECIAL STUDIES • PRAEGER SCIENTIFIC

Library of Congress Cataloging in Publication Data

Curley, Kathleen Foley.
   Word processing.

   Bibliography: p.
   Includes index.
      1. Word processing   (Office practice)
I. Title.
HF5548.115.C87   1983   652   82-18948
ISBN 0-03-062909-8

Published in 1983 by Praeger Publishers
CBS Educational and Professional Publishing
a Division of CBS Inc.
521 Fifth Avenue, New York, New York 10175, U.S.A.

© 1983 by Praeger Publishers

3456789 052 987654321

Printed in the United States of America

CONTENTS

WORD PROCESSING

1
INTRODUCTION

THE ISSUE STUDIED

Significant advances in electronics technology have created new products and made possible a wide range of new applications for existing ones. Underlying this spread of electronics technology across a broad spectrum of products has been a steady and dramatic evolution: smaller and smaller electronic components performing increasingly complex functions at ever-higher speeds and at ever-lower costs (Noyce 1977). This decrease in cost and increase in performance has promoted a widening range of applications for computer-based systems.

One of the fastest growing applications is the area of office automation, which has been brought about by advances in electronics technology and a growing need for improved office or white-collar productivity. Despite the obvious needs and apparent benefits of the technology, its diffusion and impact on white-collar productivity has remained fairly insignificant. This discrepancy between the technology's potential and its actual use is often referred to as an "implementation gap."

This study was undertaken to investigate whether such a gap exists between system potential and actual use among a sample of organizations. The primary purpose of this research was to initiate development of a practical theory of implementation for office automation technology.

Of the various office automation technologies, word processing was chosen because historically it has been the first computer-based tool in widespread use in the general office (Lodahl and Meyer 1980). Second, the highly integrated information systems envisioned for the office of the future, which incorporate linkages from text-editing machines to intelligent copiers or

1

terminal-to-terminal communications for electronic mail, all emanate from the basic word processing technology (Kleinschrod 1979).

In this study the author looked at word processing from the point of view of the user and examined how the technology was applied in different organizational settings. The findings indicate that in order to be effectively utilized, today's computer-based office automation technologies require nontraditional approaches to implementation. This is especially true in the areas of cost/benefit analysis and organizational learning. Based on extensive field research, the concept of an "intellectual technology" was developed to explain the range of implementation phenomena the author observed. This concept is then used as a basis for recommendations to managers who are concerned with the innovative use of office automation technologies to improve corporate performance.

BACKGROUND OF THE OFFICE ENVIRONMENT
AND TECHNOLOGY IMPLEMENTATION

Computer-based technologies are not new to office settings. The decade of the 1960s witnessed an explosive growth in the application of computer technology to well-structured, high-volume, and numerically based office tasks such as payroll processing, accounts payable, and purchasing (Zisman 1978). Until recently use of computerized systems was reserved for the "numbers" side of the business, with the "verbal," or prose, side of the office experiencing no real change in technology since the introduction of the typewriter in the late 1890s (Current 1954).

Between 1970 and 1980 this discrepancy in technological sophistication began to change dramatically for two reasons: sharply dropping costs of technology, and rising costs of white-collar labor.

The decline in cost and improvement in performance of electronic technology has made possible new applications for computer-based systems. In 1980 it was possible to purchase a stand-alone word processing machine, which was microprocessor based, for $7,895 (Business Week, June 30, 1980). This system has been designed for basic text editing and has a 25-line full display screen, a movable keyboard, and a 15-character-per-second printer, as well as a floppy disc memory that holds up to 100 typewritten pages. In addition the machine has a 50,000 word dictionary that will highlight misspelled words in the text. Along with these impressive price/performance features, stand-alone word processing systems have become substantially easier to use. Operating a machine such as this does not require programming or computer skills.

This decreasing cost and improved performance couples with the second major reason for the spread of such office automation technologies: the increase in the number of white-collar workers and the rising costs of paying them. Since 1960 more people have been involved in manipulating information than in growing food, manufacturing goods, or providing personal services. Employment trends for the future show rapid expansion in three job categories: professional and technical, managerial, and administrative and clerical. At the present time, 22 percent of the total work force is in office work or administrative processing (Strassmann 1980).

In addition to this occupation shift, there has been a shift in investment focus. Since 1960, economic resources have been shifted away from the production of goods and even services to the production of knowledge and information (Strassmann 1980). As these changes have occurred the white-collar or office-cost budget has been eating up more of total company resources. An average increase in office costs from 20 to 30 percent of total company costs in 1970 to 40 to 50 percent in 1975 represents a significant impact on profitability (Business Week, June 1975). Traditionally, organizations have made little investment in technology for office employees. Estimates for average capitalization per office worker range from $2,000 to about $6,000. By comparison the average capitalization per factory worker is reported to be about $25,000. In the factory this substitution of capital for labor has brought about impressive gains in productivity (Business Week, June 1975).

With white-collar payrolls making up an ever-increasing percentage of total expenses, and inflation making increased productivity an urgent need, the office is now a ripe target for automation. Yet despite the overwhelming need and apparent benefits, actual adoption and use of the technology has proceeded slowly within the general office setting.

Several reasons for the slow rate of diffusion of an apparently worthwhile technology began to appear in the popular business press under the heading of "What Not To Do" when installing new office automation technology. One often-cited reason for the apparent failure of word-processing and other office automation technologies to "catch on" was the notion that while computer-based systems had worked well where work could be automated easily, they were not suited for the general office setting. One-page letters, frequent interruptions, and "rush" jobs made the office much more of a job shop operation and therefore difficult if not impossible to automate in any significant way.

Another perceived stumbling block to the use of computer-based technologies was the proposed reorganization of the traditional office. IBM had introduced its System 6 Word Processor in the early 1970s and marketed it as a centralized approach to text management. Correspondence could be either dictated or written and sent to a central group for transcribing. This approach broke up traditional working relationships and tended to provoke resistance from executives and secretaries alike (Business Week, March 24, 1980).

In addition to this organizational resistance, the "psychological barrier" to technology surfaced as another reason for the modest success rates of a promising new technology. Monson H. Hays, Jr., President of Northern Telecom, Inc., offered the following observations:

> My feeling is that the major problem in coping with, implementing and making effective use of data and telecommunications is not going to be technological or even regulatory. It is going to be psychological and sociological — the ability of office workers, managers, to work with, understand and handle a whole different world of devices that may well change society itself (Hays 1979).

THE RESEARCH DESIGN

The failure of computer-based systems to live up to expectations is not a new phenomenon. In the field of management information systems (MIS) the implementation gap has come to be recognized as one of the major challenges confronting MIS specialists. This gap between the actual and the possible has spawned the growth of a rather extensive body of research that will be used as a basis for looking at the implementation of word processing technology.

The initial methodology within the MIS area for studying the implementation gap was the close scrutiny of user organizations in detailed case studies. These case studies then gave rise to a series of hypotheses that were tested both through survey and case analysis (Keen 1977).

Within the area of word processing no such case analysis exists. This "micro" research is important to develop clinically grounded hypotheses on why organizations have failed to fully utilize the potential of word processing technologies within office settings. Without such hypotheses, the second phase, or verification research, cannot proceed since there exists no widely known or testable model.

This study was an attempt to provide some basic research in the field of office automation by focusing on one technology: word processing and its implementation within organizational settings.

The research begins with historical case analyses in order to determine each organization's initial purchase criterion, and to examine what changes, if any, take place after the introduction of word processing technology. The information and insights gathered from the case research are then used as a basis for a survey questionnaire on the implementation of word processing technology in 30 companies.

While the focus of the research is on the user/consumer of the technology, as Tilton (1971) has noted, the diffusion process occurs on both the supply and demand sides. The producer/supply side is examined in an industry analysis to provide the reader with the necessary background to view the utilization of the technology. Industry structure has a strong influence on determining the competitive rules of the game: pricing strategies, the range of products offered, the speed with which new products will be introduced and marketed. As such, an understanding of the underlying competitive forces is an important backdrop to looking at how a technology is purchased and used, since a company's choice of products is indeed influenced by the price/performance features and technical sophistication of the products offered. These product characteristics are in turn influenced by the technological state of the art, consumer demand, evolutionary stage of the product (Abernathy & Utterback 1978) as well as the competitive forces at work within the industry itself. This analysis will provide the reader with an understanding of the relative advantage that the technology offers to buyers in terms of price/performance characteristics.

The industry analysis itself was conducted according to the techniques described in <u>Competitive Strategy: Techniques for Analyzing Industries and Competition</u> (Porter 1980). The author gathered data both from published and clinical sources on the following topics:

1. History of product/market development. What were the characteristics of the initial products offered? Who were the first players on the market? What were the characteristics of the firms who first entered the market?

2. Product lines. What is the range of products offered now? What are their characteristics? How have the products now available changed since the first marketing of word processing equipment?

3. Growth rates and trends. What is the market rate of growth in terms of dollar volume and units sold? What seem to be the future trends in terms of type of equipment sold and total market size?

4. Marketing and selling. Are there identifiable market segments for word processing equipment? How do vendor firms manage their sales effort to focus on key markets?

5. Innovation. What are the technological innovations that have occurred in the industry? Are there other types of innovations, marketing, distribution, that seem important?

6. Competition/competitive strategies. What are the competitive strategies of the major vendor firms? Who are their target markets? What are their relative market shares? What do the various vendor firms see as their own areas of competence?

For the purpose of comparison with research done by International Data Corporation (IDC) the largest information gathering group in the area of office automation, I have used its definition of a word processor as "any electronic device which provides for the storing, editing, and reproduction of textual information (International Data Corporation is source; hereafter referred to as IDC). Within this broad definition IDC used the following categories:

1. Electronic Typewriters. The low end of the market consists of an automated typewriter with memory of 1,000 characters of less and no removable media. The high end would include machines that do have removable media as well as a larger memory.

2. Stand-Alone Nondisplay. These machines were among the first word processors sold. Originally they stored data on magnetic tapes or cards. There are some machines in this category that store information on discs and are still sold, but in general they have been replaced by the easier-to-use display units.

3. Stand-Alone Single Line Display. These machines are generally called "thin window" units, because they are equipped with a small screen that displays one or two lines of text. Information is usually stored on discs.

4. Stand-Alone Display. This machine includes keyboard, separate printer, and video screen. The editing is performed on a screen and memory may be floppy disc, diskette, or hard disc.

5. Clustered Systems. A multiterminal configuration attached to a Central Processing Unit (CPU) that handles communications and maintains a separate document base.

6. Hybrid Systems. This category usually includes display units combining data and word processing capability. Usually equipped with a microprocessor so they have their own intelligence.

7. Time Sharing. Purchasing the text-editing power of a CPU through a dumb terminal on a pay-as-you-go basis.

OVERVIEW OF THE CHAPTERS

Chapter 2 presents a review of the relevant literature from the fields of management of technology, management information systems, and organizational change. This review provides the basis for the conceptual framework and the methodology presented in greater detail in Chapter 3. Chapter 4 is an analysis of the word processing industry between 1964 and 1979, gathered from published sources and interviews with key personnel at the various vendor firms. Chapter 5 details the field research at three case sites and presents an analysis of the results. In Chapter 6 the survey data gathered from 21 responding companies are presented and analyzed. Finally, Chapter 7 presents the hypotheses generated from the field research and discusses their implications for managers and researchers.

2
REVIEW OF THE LITERATURE

This chapter examines available research findings that seem relevant to understanding the process of implementing a new technology within an organizational setting. I have brought together literature from three separate disciplines — management of technology, management information systems, and organizational change — in an effort to synthesize approaches and provide a holistic view of the diffusion/implementation process. Each area by itself tells only part of the story. Exploring the dynamic relationship that exists between supply/demand and between initial adoption/ongoing utilization has provided a rich framework for understanding the implementation of word processing technology.

This literature review also presents the various explanations why an apparently worthwhile technology may fail to become widely diffused or live up to its expected potential.

BRINGING TECHNOLOGY TO THE MARKET

In examining the process of how technological innovation occurs to create new products and bring them to widespread use, researchers in the area of management of technology have identified factors that appear to be important in determining the rate at which these innovations come to the market and are subsequently diffused. Two of the factors found to be significant are: market structure/competitive environment and evolutionary stage of the product.

The earliest suggestion that there was a correlation between market structure/competitive environment and the rate of innovation grew out of Joseph Schumpeter's (1942) hypothesis that "in

8

the absence of uncommitted surplusses, the undertaking of risky and uncertain innovation activity would not occur." He predicted that "the trail of innovative activity leads to the doors of big companies not competing in perfect markets."

Schumpeter reasoned that perceived risk was an important attribute in determining a firm's willingness to innovate and that only firms with substantial resources to absorb the financial risk (that is, surplusses) and the likelihood of capturing greater than marginal profits (that is, monopoly or oligopoly profits) would be motivated to invest in innovation.

Since Schumpeter's work first appeared, many studies have been undertaken to examine the relationship among market structure, firm size, and the rate of innovation.

Markham (1964) found that up to a certain size of firm, measured by total sales, innovational effort as measured by research and development expenses as a percent of sales does increase more than proportionately. After this threshold size level is reached, innovational effort does not increase and may actually decline.

Scherer (1970) conducted a study of patents in 352 companies across 14 industries to examine whether patenting increased more than proportionately with firm size. His findings suggested that size of firm could not be correlated with innovative activity. What was needed for innovation and its subsequent diffusion, Scherer suggested, was a subtle blend of competition and monopoly. That is, some types of innovations seemed to be more likely in a highly competitive market while others were more likely to take place in large firms in oligopolistic markets.

The idea that "type of innovation" was correlated with market structure/competitive environment was further explored by Abernathy and Utterback (1978) in their work on the technology life cycle.

Abernathy and Utterback found that there were certain patterns of innovation that could be discerned over time within a given product technology. Their unit of analysis (called a productive unit) focused on a specific product and the process used to make it. Their findings showed that a productive unit's capability to support innovation depended on its stage of development. They demonstrated that the character of innovation and the organizational structure of an enterprise changed as it matured from a small technology-based firm to a major high-volume producer.

The technology life cycle concept provides a framework for looking at the process of technological innovation in light of the evolutionary stages it outlines. Referring to Figure 2.1, the "fluid" pattern of organizational structure with its emphasis on product innovation is associated with the early stages of the product's development. The transitional stage, which is ushered

FIGURE 2.1
Innovation and Transition in Productive Units

RELATIVE LEVELS OF PRODUCT AND PROCESS INNOVATION THROUGHOUT THE FLUID/SPECIFIC SPECTRUM

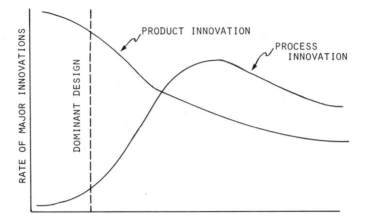

	FLUID PATTERN	TRANSITIONAL PATTERN	SPECIFIC PATTERN
Competitive emphasis on	Functional product performance	Product variation	Cost reduction
Innovation stimulated by	Information on users' needs and users' technical inputs	Opportunities created by expanding internal technical capability	Pressure to reduce cost and improve quality
Predominant type of innovation	Frequent major changes in products	Major process changes required by rising volume	Incremental for product and process, with cumulative improvement in productivity and quality
Product line	Diverse, often including custom designs	Includes at least one product design stable enough to have significant production volume	Mostly undifferentiated standard products
Production processes	Flexible and inefficient; major changes easily accommodated	Becoming more rigid, with changes occurring in major steps	Efficient, capital-intensive, and rigid: cost of change is high
Equipment	General-purpose, requiring highly skilled labor	Some subprocesses automated, creating "islands of automation'	Special-purpose, mostly automatic with labor tasks mainly monitoring and control
Materials	Inputs are limited to generally-availavel materials	Specialized materials may be demanded from some suppliers	Specilized materials will be demanded; if not available, vertical integration will be extensive
Plant	Small-scale, located near user or source of technology	General-purpose with specialized sections	Large-scale, highly specific to particular products
Organizational control is	Informal and entrepreneurial	Through liaison relationships, project and task groups	Through emphasis on structure, goals and rules

Source: From Abernathy and Utterback (1978). Reprinted with permission from Technology Review, copyright 1978.

10

in by the emergence of a dominant product design, is associated with increased competition on the marketing side and process innovation and an emphasis on increasing volume at lowered costs on the manufacturing side. The "specific" pattern corresponds to the product's mature stage where emphasis is on cost reduction and maintenance of existing market shares through tighter control and a more rigid organizational structure. Abernathy and Utterback present the following summary of their findings:

> We assert that technological opportunities, improvements and additions to existing product lines, and a high degree of research and development will be characteristic of firms in transition. Such firms are expected to place increasing emphasis on product differentiation and cost reduction. Most major product innovation is expected to occur when a firm's product and process technology are fluid, and to be market stimulated, rather than when it spends most heavily on research and to be technology stimulated. Firms in transition will also be most likely to see opportunities for and to derive benefits from research and development, and thus to invest heavily in formal research and engineering departments. This is consistent with various findings that the largest firms in many industries (those having the most highly standardized products and specific process technology) are not the most research and development intensive in terms of R and D expenditures related to market share. Rather it is the medium-sized firms (those in transition) that spend relatively the greatest amount on Research and Development.
>
> The fact that small new enterprises, or larger firms entering a new business, are believed to introduce a disproportionate share of major product innovation is also a finding that is consistent with the model.
>
> The proposed model represents a departure from much of the previous research on technological innovation in that it seeks to understand technological progress in holistic form, over time, as a dynamic relationship among many variables, rather than to attempt to isolate independent effects of individual factors at a given time. It raises a set of new hypotheses on which research has yet to be undertaken. These follow from the idea that technology and other characteristics of organization, market, and production process must be matched, and that successful technological advance has a generalized pattern.

This generalized pattern that Abernathy and Utterback discovered was that the evolution of technology occurs in predictable and identifiable stages. Thus they examined diffusion from the producer/supply side and found it to be an evolutionary process that exhibits certain recurring patterns.

Their work opened a new area of research that looked at technological change as a dynamic relationship, occurring over time, among the variables of technology, market, organization, and production process. Successful management of innovation therefore required an appropriate matching of these variables as they change over the life cycle of the product. Thus their hypothesis suggests that no single organizational size, market structure, or product characteristic can be associated with success, as earlier writers had indicated. Success depends instead on a mix of technological and competitive factors that are continually changing. We will use their model as a basis for examining the evolution of word processing technology and the competitive forces at work within this market.

Other researchers — Rogers and Shoemaker (1962, 1971) and Marquis (1969) — in the area of management of technology focused on the demand or buyer side of the market in order to learn what factors affected the decision to adopt an innovation. Since Abernathy and Utterback had suggested that market stimulus was a key factor in determining the success of an innovation, the research of Rogers and Shoemaker, and others, provides an important complement to innovation literature.

THE PURCHASE DECISION: HOW BUYERS DECIDE TO ADOPT AN INNOVATION

Rogers and Shoemaker (1971) provide the most comprehensive review and integration of the empirical research on user adoption of innovations prior to 1971. The impetus for their work is described by the following quote:

> The rate at which empirical results have been adequately digested and integrated into theoretical formulations has not kept pace. If we continue to generate studies at even the present rate without a major leap forward in terms of integrative theory, we shall drown in our own data.

Indeed their research did contribute substantially to developing a more comprehensive theory of diffusion. Prior to their work, a controversy existed over what factors were important in determining the rate of diffusion of U.S. farming innovations. There was particular disagreement over whether adoption of new farming methods was more influenced by characteristics of the innovation, or by the educational level of the farmer. Rogers and Shoemaker argued that the characteristics of the innovation were more important, and they were able to identify five basic characteristics that, when viewed from the perspective of the potential users, would determine the likelihood of an innovation's acceptance: relative advantage, compatibility, complexity, trialability, and observability.

In reviewing 11 different experimental studies, Rogers and Shoemaker found that these five attributes explained between 49 and 87 percent of the variance in the rate of innovation adoption. Summaries of these experiments are presented under each of the five attribute headings.

Relative Advantage

Zvi Griliches (1957), an economist, conducted research indicating that the lag in the use of hybrid corn could be explained by the varying profitability associated with initial use. Thus where profits were large and clear cut, changeover was rapid. He was able to explain 30 percent of the variance in the rate of adoption of hybrid corn based on the one variable of profitability. Griliches found that the relative advantage of the new corn in economic terms was the most significant factor in determining whether farmers used the hybrid seed.

Studies by Mansfield (1971) and Scherer (1970) lent support to the hypothesis that relative advantage was an important if not primary determinant of whether an innovation would be adopted, particularly in an industrial market (Utterback 1974).

Compatibility

The compatibility of an innovation with existing processes, norms, and values was seen to have a major impact on its rate of acceptance in many of the studies that also highlighted the importance of relative advantage. Kivlin (1960) and Fliegel and Kivlin (1962) found compatibility to be the second most significant determinant of adoption rate after relative advantage.

Apodaca's (1952) research on the use of hybrid corn by Spanish American farmers in New Mexico showed that it was possible for an incompatibility between an innovation and a potential adopter to overshadow economic advantage.

In Apodaca's study, 33 of 84 growers in one village planted at least some hybrid corn in 1946. Their yields were double the yields from old seeds. In the following year, over half of the villagers planted hybrid corn. By 1949, however, use of the hybrid corn had fallen off considerably and only 3 percent of the growers planted the seed. The village farmers had discontinued their use of the corn because their wives felt the hybrid had a strange flavor and did not "hang together well" for tortillas. The social norms favored the old variety rather than the hybrid. The hybrid corn was incompatible with existing tastes and cooking procedures and for this reason was not adopted despite its obvious economic advantage.

In general, the diffusion research has not focused on the longer-term impacts of an adoption decision as does Apodaca's study. However, "compatibility" is a characteristic of an innovation that surfaces both here and in the organizational change literature as an important determinant of successful diffusion.

Complexity

In addition to relative advantage and compatibility, several researchers (Kivlin 1960; Singh 1966; Petrini 1966) found that complexity — that is, the degree to which an innovation is perceived by potential adopters as difficult to understand or use — was more likely to influence the rate of adoption than any other characteristic of the innovation except relative advantage (Rogers and Shoemaker 1962-1971; Cale 1979).

Trialability

Similarly, many of these same researchers found that trialability — the degree to which the potential adopter is allowed to experiment with an innovation prior to total commitment — has a significant positive effect on the rate of adoption.

Observability

Finally, Hruschka and Rheinwald (1965) found that those innovations made visible through demonstrations by German "pilot farmers" diffused more widely than less visible innovations. Thus, some highly advantageous, but not very visible, innovations spread at a slower rate than other less advantageous but more visible innovations.

In their review of the diffusion research, Rogers and Shoemaker (1971) reiterated that the perceived attributes of the innovation were more important than the characteristics of the adopting population to the spread of a new product or idea.

Perceived Risk

Another perceived attribute of an innovation — risk — has been examined by a number of other researchers (Scherer 1970; Masbeth and Ray 1974) to determine its importance in explaining the rate of adoption. Rogers and Shoemaker did not list risk as one of the "primary" attributes influencing the diffusion of an innovation as they felt it overlapped significantly with several of the other five attributes, especially relative advantage, compatibility, and complexity.

Nevertheless, in a study done for the British government to examine the intercountry diffusion of industrial processes, Nasbeth and Ray found that the size of a required investment and its perceived risk were important factors in determining the speed with which an innovation would be adopted.

Other researchers such as Bower (1972) and Scherer (1970) also identified perceived risk as an important factor in determining resource allocation for new products or processes.

Summary

In examining diffusion from the demand or user side and principally as a single decision point, we can summarize the research findings as follows: The rate of speed at which an innovation is adopted is determined in large part by the perceived attributes of the innovation. We will use this finding as a basis for examining the perceived attributes of word processing technology.

In the following section we will review the literature on management information systems and organizational change that focuses on the implementation of technologies such as word processing within organizational settings.

UTILIZING COMPUTER-BASED SYSTEMS

Over the past three decades, growth in the use of computer-based systems has been explosive (Cale 1979). Increasingly, organizations have come to depend upon these systems to provide a variety of support activities vital to the operation of the organization. In 1971 G. Anthony Gorry and Michael Scott-Morton suggested a framework for understanding the use of MIS within organizations. They maintained that as systems proliferated, there was a need to develop a coherent way of examining the process of technology diffusion that was occurring. The motivation for looking at the intraorganizational diffusion of MIS technology was that such knowledge was thought to be a useful and necessary input to systems designers.

Drawing on the work of Simon (1960) and Anthony (1965) Gorry and Scott-Morton's article focused on the different types of decision-making processes in organizations. They believed that a basic understanding of managerial decision making was a prerequisite for effective systems design and implementation. As a framework for understanding different types of decision making, they used the following classification of managerial activity in their research:

Strategic Planning: The process of deciding on objectives of the organization, on changes in those objectives, the resources used to attain them, and on the policies that govern the acquisition, use, and disposition of these resources.

Management Control: The process by which managers assure that resources are obtained and used effectively and efficiently in the accomplishment of the organization's objectives.

Operational Control: The process of assuring that specific tasks are carried out effectively and efficiently.

Gorry and Scott-Morton reasoned that these different categories of managerial activity required different types of decision-making processes and therefore would need to be supported by different types of information systems. In describing these categories they made the following observations:

We recognize, as does Anthony, that the boundaries between these three categories are often not clear. In spite of their limitations and uncertainties, however, we have found the categories useful in the analysis of information system activities. For example, if we consider the information requirements of these three activities, we can see that they are very different from one another. Further, this difference is not simply a matter of aggregation, but one of fundamental character of the information needed by managers in these areas.

Strategic planning is concerned with setting broad policies and goals for the organization. As a result, the relationship of the organization to its environment is a central matter of concern. Also the nature of the activity is such that predictions about the future are particularly important. In general then, we can say that the information needed by strategic planners is aggregate information, and obtained mainly from sources external to the organization itself. Both the scope and variety of the information are quite large, but the requirements for accuracy are not particularly stringent. Finally the non-routine nature of the strategic planning process means that the demands for this information occur infrequently.

The information needs for the operational control area stand in sharp contrast to those of strategic planning. The task orientation of operational control requires information of a well-defined and narrow scope. This information is quite detailed and arises largely from sources within the organization. Very frequent use is made of this information, and it must therefore be accurate.

The information requirements for management control fall between the extremes for operational control and strategic planning. In addition, it is important to recognize that much of the information relevant to management control is obtained through the process of interpersonal interaction.

Gorry and Scott-Morton link these views of managerial activity with the decision-making concepts originally advanced by Simon (1960):

Decisions are programmed to the extent that they are repetitive and routine, to the extent that a definite procedure has been worked out for handling them so that they don't have to be treated "de novo" each time they occur. . . . Decisions are nonprogrammed to the extent that they are novel, unstructured, and consequential. There is no cut and dried method of handling the problem because it hasn't arisen before or because its precise nature and structure are elusive or complex, or because it is so important that it deserves a custom-tailored treatment. . . . By "nonprogrammed" I mean a response where the system has no specific procedure to deal with situations like the one at hand, but must fall back on whatever general capacity it has for intelligent, adaptive, problem oriented action.

Gorry and Scott-Morton substitute the terms "structured" and "nonstructured" for "programmed" and "nonprogrammed" as these terms imply less dependence on the computer and more dependence on the basic character of the problem-solving activity. By combining the ideas of Simon and Anthony, the authors have constructed a framework that highlights the purposes and problems of information systems activity in organizations (see Figure 2.2).

FIGURE 2.2
Gorry and Scott-Morton Information Systems Framework

	Operational Control	Management Control	Strategic Planning
Structured	Accounts Receivable	Budget Analysis-Engineered	Tank Fleet Mix
	Order Entry	Short-Term Forecasting	Warehouse and Factory Location
	Inventory Control		
Semistructured	Production Scheduling	Variance Analysis Overall Budget	Merger and Acquisitions
	Cash Management	Budget Preparation	New Product Planning
Unstructured	PERT/COST Systems	Sales and Production	R&D Planning

In describing their framework, the authors suggest that decisions above the dotted line shown in Figure 2.2 are largely structured and require "structured decision systems" to support them. An example of a "structured decision system" might be the use of the classical economic order quantity (EOQ) formula on a straightforward inventory control problem. That is, it is possible to specify algorithms, or decision rules, that will allow the user to find the problem, design alternative solutions, and select the best solution.

Decisions described below the dotted line in Figure 2.2 are largely unstructured, and their supporting information systems are "decision support systems." Work in these unstructured areas is much more involved with model development and judgment rather than the use of optimization formulas.

In addition, Gorry and Scott-Morton suggest that the line separating structured from unstructured decisions is evolutionary in nature, and therefore moving all the time. That is,

> as we improve our understanding of a particular decision, we can make it more structured and allow the system to take care of it, freeing the manager for other tasks. For example, in previous years the inventory reordering system decision in most organizations was made by a well-paid member of middle management. It was a decision that involved a high degree of skill and could have a significant effect on the profits of the organization. Today this decision has moved from the unstructured operational control area to the structured. We have a set of decision rules (the EOQ formula) which on average do a better job for the standard items that most human decision makers.

The framework suggests that different kinds of managerial activity require different kinds of system support. It also suggests that over time managers will learn to structure tasks to take advantage of system capability while freeing up their own time for more unstructured problem solving.

As the use of computer-based systems continued to grow, there appeared a growing body of literature concerned with the gap between systems potential and actual use. This gap between technical capability and actual practice began to be investigated under the heading of "implementation research." The concept of implementation as a legitimate area for academic research was a new one; as Keen (1977) points out, one of the first books to explicitly address implementation as an area of operations research was published in 1970. Throughout that decade much additional research and data gathering was done by a variety of investigators from different academic and managerial backgrounds on the implementation problem (Lucas 1978; Argyris 1970).

Despite this flurry of research activity on implementation, the state of knowledge in the field remains roughly where the research on purchaser decision making was prior to the work of Rogers and Shoemaker. That is, there exists a large data base in the form of both case studies and survey data, but as yet the implementation research suffers from the lack of a cohesive theory that would provide a framework for binding together the empirical research.

In addition, implementation research suffers from a definitional problem: What is implementation? When is a system said to be implemented? What is successful implementation? Earlier diffusion research reviewed at the beginning of this chapter focused on adoption of an innovation mostly as a single decision point, identifiable and clearly defined. While researchers in the area of MIS implementation would probably be unanimous in their agreement that implementation goes beyond the single decision point, how far beyond would be a matter of contention.

Yet even without a comprehensive theory or a standard definition, implementation remains an important concern both to managers and researchers. The obvious benefits from organizations learning to manage the utilization of computer-based technology to its fullest potential are enormous. In an effort to review and synthesize the variety of research studies on implementation, Keen (1977) divided the available research into seven major categories based on the general character or approach of the study. Examination of the strengths and weaknesses of each is summarized here:

Failure literature. This is the oldest approach to implementation research and aims mainly at consciousness raising among technical professionals, redirecting their attention from design to delivery by pointing to the lessons of unsuccessful projects. Frequently the literature points out how models that were technically well designed turned out to be embarrassing failures as a result of inattention to behavioral issues. The failure literature clearly lacks a single or unifying framework for analysis, and the issues raised by recounting various disasters cannot be generalized or directly tested. Nonetheless, the failure literature did provide a useful service in alerting systems designers to the gap between technical feasibility and actual practice.

Mutual Understanding. This theme underlies most of the research on differences in cognitive style between managers and analysts. It was generally hypothesized that such differences in cognitive style led operations researchers to generate products that were not compatible with the problem-solving process of most managers. The principal problem with this line of research is that it deals with only one aspect of the implementation problem and thus is difficult to operationalize, and it provides no prescriptions for action.

User-Centered Research. Like the mutual understanding school of thought, this area of research focuses on understanding the style, behavior, and needs of the user/manager. User satisfaction is the measure of success, and the emphasis is on designing systems that will be tailored to meet these needs. Keen makes the interesting point that user-centered research essentially argues for tailoring operations research/management science projects to fit the individual users, thereby avoiding the need for change on their part. In instances where such tailoring is impossible, user-centered research provides little help to the implementor faced with the problem.

Factor Study. The general approach in this line of research was to identify the variables that might be relevant to implementation by building questionnaires and sampling a range of implementation efforts. The responses were then clustered through multivariate techniques, such as factor analysis, to identify variables that could be strongly correlated with success and failure. The assumption behind the factor study was that there were absolute factors that could be identified with success and failure. Yet the research results do not seem to bear out the underlying assumption. Ginzberg's (1975) analysis shows that of the 140 factors identified in 14 studies, only 3 appear in 4 or more reports and 73 percent appear in only 1.

Organizational Factors Research. This research examines organizational issues in implementation mainly through longitudinal studies. This category of research is fairly mature and has accumulated enough data to be able to formalize and strengthen the underlying paradigm that implementation occurs in evolutionary stages that have distinct and identifiable characteristics.

Contingency Literature. This research draws on many categories of study to suggest contingent strategies for managing the implementation process. It consciously opposes the factor study approach, arguing that there are no fixed rules for implementation. Because of its "contingent" nature, the concepts are neither generalizable nor prescriptive.

Social Change Research. This area draws on a strong tradition of work in the social sciences. It is more comprehensive than the mutual understanding, user-centered, or factor studies research. it uses the longitudinal perspective of the organizational factors research, but it is more prescriptive in that it addresses the question of how one moves through the various evolutionary stages.

Keen suggests that the overall aim of implementation research should be to provide explanations in a format that permits making normative recommendations. The research therefore needs to be comparative. For this reason Keen asserts that a suspension of effort on failure, contingency, and factor studies is likely to occur.

The mutual understanding and the user-centered research streams reflect the earlier bias in MIS efforts to tailor both the hardware and software to the particular needs of the end user. However, the increasing cost of personnel required to design systems, and write programs, has brought about the widespread use of "canned" programs and systems (Gremillion 1979). This means that extensive modification and tailoring of the system must be minimized, or users themselves must begin to develop basic programming skills so that they can make system modifications on an individual basis (Lucas 1978). In either case, the design and implementation emphasis shifts from understanding and addressing user needs to providing flexible technology that can be implemented within an organizational setting.

Radnor et al. (1970) and later Nolan (1979) used a similar organizational approach to identify, through longitudinal studies, distinct stages in the utilization of management information systems by examining selected aspects of organizational structure and procedure. This diffusion or evolution began with a "missionary" phase, in which the MIS unit actively sought to sell its services, leading to a "contagion" stage, in which demand for such service grew dramatically, through to "institutionalization" of the service. Nolan's work (1974, 1979) suggests that the researcher can view this process by focusing on the changes that occur in the following four variables: technology, portfolio of technology use, organizational structure, and control system.

Because of this organizational emphasis, the organizational factors and the social change research have emerged as the most promising constructs for future implementation research. The organizational factors research has produced the hypothesis that there is a life cycle pattern associated with the long-term implementation of MIS. As Keen (1977) notes, "the Life Cycle effect is one of the few clearly supported and generalizable conclusions from implementation research."

In the field investigation I examined to what extent this "life cycle effect" could be observed in the use of word processing systems.

STRATEGIES FOR CHANGE: MANAGING THE
INTRODUCTION OF NEW TECHNOLOGY

The organizational change literature provides a perspective for viewing implementation as a dynamic process involving the introduction of a technical change into an existing social system.

Beer (1980) and Kotter (1978) state that organizations need to look at the introduction of technology as a change strategy requiring careful planning. They suggest that

$$C = A + B + D/x$$

The degree of change (C) depends on the strength of (A) the dissatisfaction of the status quo, (B) the desirability of the perceived goal, and (D) the availability of practical steps. All need to be greater than (X) the perceived costs, both financial and psychological, of making the change. Elaborating on the formula, Beer suggests that successful management of change requires:

Management Commitment. Key managers must be intellectually and emotionally committed to the new technology. Otherwise they cannot provide leadership for the change effort.

Political Support. While top managers need not be intellectually and emotionally committed they do need to provide political support for the key managers involved in carrying out the change process.

Resources. Key managers must have sufficient resources (financial, technical, human) in order to be successful at managing the change process.

Lewin's (1958) framework is a prescription for bringing about organizational change through the following processes:

Unfreezing. Alteration of the forces acting on the individual or social unit such that his/her equilibrium is disturbed and he/she moves toward needing rather than resisting change. As a practical matter, unfreezing involves getting people to examine and question their present way of doing things.

Change. The presentation of the change program. Changing to a new system demands a great deal of organizational learning, which often involves bringing about changes in the overall culture of the organization as well as the specific organizational variables involved (Argyris 1970).

Refreezing. The integration of the change into the personality and ongoing activities of the individual or organization. Refreezing involves making organizational policies and procedures consistent with the behavior needed under the new system.

An expansion of this scheme, based on Kolb and Frohman's (1970) definition of an organizational change process, is used by a number of researchers. Their model includes five stages:

Scouting. Matching the capabilities of the change agent/ analysis to the demands of the problem.

Entry. Building a felt need for change; defining goals in operational terms; setting up a contract for change; recognizing and responding to resistance; ensuring realistic mutual expectations.

Diagnosis, Planning, and Action. Designing and operationalizing the change program. These stages correspond closely to the technical conceptional design.

Evaluation. Monitoring progress in terms of the plans and contract defined at Entry and determining when the system is "complete."

Termination. The integration of the system into the organization so that it is no longer dependent on the consultant/analyst but is self sustaining.

The definition of success implicit in most of the organizational change literature is the institutionalization of the change itself — in other words, building a new set of relationships among the key organizational variables. The life cycle concept proposed by Gorry and Scott-Morton, Radnor et al., and Nolan would alert us to the fact that no initial design is ever perfect and that "refreezing" in Lewin's terms does not refer to "freezing" the new system's design or procedures. No organization ever stays the same for long, and constant revision of systems seems inevitable. Nevertheless, the organizational change literature does provide a useful set of recommendations for implementing a new technology within an organizational setting.

SUMMARY

The research findings reviewed in this chapter form the basis of our understanding of the implementation issue to be investigated. Each of these three sections contributes insight into the dynamic relationships that exist in bringing an innovation to the market, diffusing it, and subsequently implementing it within an organizational setting. These findings are the foundation of the conceptual framework of this investigation of word processing implementation.

3
CONCEPTUAL FRAMEWORK AND RESEARCH DESIGN

Using the literature as background, the research design starts with an examination of the underlying technological and competitive factors that influence which word processing products are made available to buyers. The next stage investigates how a sample of organizations decides to purchase and subsequently utilize word processing technology, and looks at the impact of the technology on the organization's structure, the tasks it performs, and the people who work in it.

At this point the question of an implementation gap can be addressed. Does the research indicate an observable gap between system potential and actual use? If so, is this something regularly observed in utilizing word processing technology or does it appear to be limited to a small number of users?

Another basic research question is whether utilization of word processing technology follows an evolutionary pattern similar to what researchers observed in the MIS area. Finally, the change strategies employed by a sample of firms are studied in an effort to identify the most successful.

DEVELOPING A CONCEPTUAL FRAMEWORK

The research is exploratory in nature. That is, it is designed to generate hypotheses rather than verify an existing paradigm. Since the study is an exploration of an observed phenomenon, rather than an experimental test of a model, we are more concerned with description than prescription. As a first step toward developing an implementation theory, we need to be able to describe what actually happens. We can then begin to analyze these experiences to determine if there are patterns of decision

25

making, change strategies, or utilization procedures that seem to work better than others. From the descriptive data we begin the development of a normative theory for the purchase and implementation of office automation technology.

It should be noted here that while the research is exploratory and designed to develop a hypothesis, an observer cannot realistically go into a field setting without some idea of what to look at and what to look for. In this way a conceptual framework provides a way of looking at and sorting information.

It is not a formal "hypothesis," but rather an investigator's informed hunch about what to look for, based upon the experience and research of others about the nature of the problem. The construction and use of a conceptual framework is what separates exploratory research from mere journalism. The framework itself is continually reevaluated, revised, and added to throughout the course of the actual field research.

Finally the investigator's first-hand experiences, sifted through this framework, together with research done by previous investigators, is welded together to form a formal hypothesis, "Ho," or a set of hypotheses, which other researchers can then use to view similar phenomena.

In this study of word processing diffusion and implementation in organizations, the following research questions directed the data gathering:

Is there an observable gap between system potential and actual use? Was this observed in isolated cases or regularly?

To what extent does the evolution of the technology work to close the implementation gap? Does this evolutionary process affect how users decide to purchase and utilize the technology?

Does the use of word processing equipment follow an evolutionary pattern similar to that observed by other researchers in the area of MIS? Did experience with the technology bring about better use of the system's potential?

Do organizations evolve from being users of word processing to use a broader range of office automation technologies?

Do organizations learn from their experience in data processing?

DESIGNING THE FIELD RESEARCH

We know from the management of technology literature that the diffusion of new products and ideas is affected by market structure/competitive environment and the evolutionary stage of the product.

We began the field research by examining the development and evolution of word processing technology itself. Could we determine the evolutionary stage of the product? What were the competitive characteristics of the market itself? What is the market rate of growth? What seem to be future trends in terms of type of equipment sold and total market size?

This information was used to identify the relative advantage the technology offered to buyers, and to examine whether the evolutionary stage of the product had an effect on the implementation process. We looked at the extent to which changes in the technology had an impact on how it was used.

DEFINING SUCCESSFUL IMPLEMENTATION

Next we observed the process of technology implementation in a sample of organizations and addressed the question of whether there appeared to be an observable gap between system potential and actual use. In order to do this we first had to tackle one of the thorniest issues in implementation research: What defines success? An "implementation gap" exists only to the extent that we can define and observe a difference between a system's potential and its actual use. The fiascos described in the failure literature clearly represent some degree of nonimplementation, yet the positive definitions vary widely.

Research that has focused on user behavior and satisfaction has tended to equate implementation success with whether the product was actually used. At the other extreme, research that has focused on organizational behavior has tended to equate implementation success with long-term strategies for change. From this view, the product or individual user is less relevant to success than the process; the organizational system may be obsolete by the time the change is institutionalized within the organization and "success" is finally achieved.

Keen (1977) recommends that success be defined in terms of intent; thus the measure of success of the implementation effort depends on its intended level of adoption. He distinguishes between two types of settings in studying "implementation":

- Fully Defined Settings: Where the intention of the project is reasonably clear so that the extent to which it meets its aims can be assessed; in this situation, the definition of "success" is intrinsic, and criteria for evaluation apparent.
- Undefined Settings: Where there is a clear initiation of the project but insufficient definition of operational goals to be able to relate outcome to intent.

Keen then argues that only "fully defined" settings would insure a comparative data base for implementation research. The emphasis on intent as part of evaluation helps facilitate the process of deriving "prescriptions from a descriptive program of research."

Keen raises a valid point. A comparative study of different implementation efforts is impossible if researchers cannot agree on what is being implemented or what defines success.

His framework of the "fully defined" setting is attractive because of its operational clarity and simplicity. There is, however, a major drawback with this approach to defining implementation success: The problem of identifying organizations with ambitious goals as "failures" if actual performance falls short of expectations. Organizations with "low" expectations and goals then could be classified as "successes" at a lower level of performance. This approach would seem to hinder the development of a comparative data base.

Much of the early "failure literature" described, in an anecdotal manner, the fact that some companies seemed to "do better" than others at implementing systems. What is really needed for comparative analysis is some definition of success that can be used to clarify what "doing better" means.

To be useful, the concept of implementation success must be applied across settings, not just within an organization's framework of intent. A generic definition of success must include some way of assessing relative performance.

Within the area of office automation, there appears to be a growing consensus that "successful" automation means going beyond the simple factory-like measures of paper output. The reason for pushing the concept of success beyond this level lies in the basic economics of office automation itself.

While much has been written about the rising costs of processing paper and hiring secretarial help, the major components of office costs are the salaries of professional and managerial workers. Secretarial costs make up only 25 percent of total office costs, while the costs of managers and professionals make up the other 75 percent (Connell 1981). Typing activity, which is the task most frequently supported by office automation technologies, actually accounts for only 1.2 percent of U.S. white-collar business costs. Therefore productivity gains in the typing area have only a marginal impact on overall office expenses.

Essentially,the activities of managers and professionals involve the communication of information. Until office automation is made to address the communication function of managers and professionals it will fail to increase the productivity of office operations significantly. Major gains come from making the technology go beyond the electronic mechanization of tasks to the overall automation of the way a business works.

This concept is supported by a variety of researchers from different backgrounds. Paul Strassmann (1980) writes:

> The office of the future is a concept revolutionary to the development of our post-industrial society because it can potentially redefine how the largest part of our working population functions. This concept should therefore not be viewed simply as a means for overcoming existing technological limitations; it should be seen as a restructuring of the thinking and working methods of professionals, managers, and administrators. . . . The idea that new technological means will by themselves produce structural changes in information management is a mirage. Although low cost technological capability is an absolute precondition for greater productivity of knowledge . . . , increased understanding of how information can be defined and channeled is the essential challenge.

Zisman (1978) makes a similar point when he suggests that the office of the future is likely to evolve from an early stage where emphasis is on the "mechanization" of tasks to a mature stage where a variety of office technologies are integrated to support a broad range of communications activity.

Other writers, Carlisle (1981), Connell (1981), and Lodahl (1980), have also suggested that successful implementation of office automation technology must go beyond the simple notion of output efficiency to include increased effectiveness and managerial support.

There are two important concepts that emerge from this literature:

1. The real payoff for successful implementation comes from using the technology as a catalyst for restructuring the thinking and working methods of managers and professionals. Therefore, defining "implementation success" requires a longitudinal perspective where the goal is greater productivity through the restructuring of managerial and professional work.

2. Underlying this long-term evolutionary process is the organizational learning necessary to successfully implement the system. In trying to determine what the characteristics of this learning are for users of word processing equipment, we can get some assistance from previous research done in the field of data processing. Richard Nolan (1974, 1979) has tracked the implementation of data processing systems in various organizations over the past ten years. His findings suggest that for the data processing application of computer technology, stages of learning exhibit specific characteristics shown in Figure 3.1.

FIGURE 3.1

Six Stages of Data Processing Growth

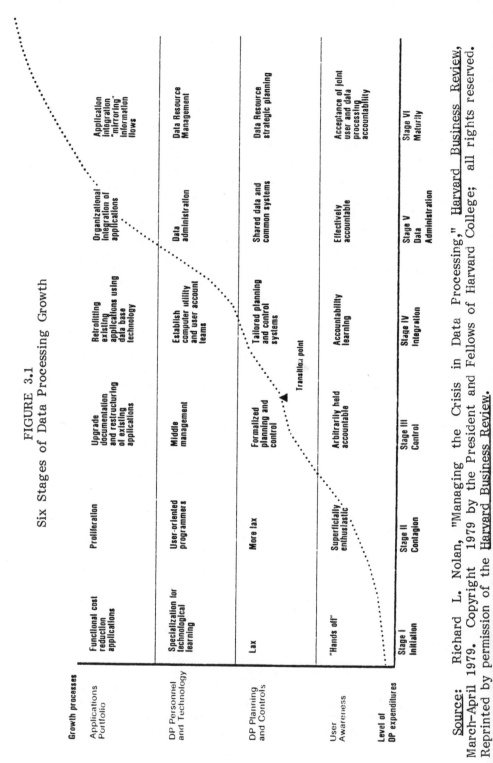

Growth processes						
Applications Portfolio	Functional cost reduction applications	Proliferation	Upgrade documentation and restructuring of existing applications	Retrofitting existing applications using data base technology	Organizational integration of applications	Application integration "mirroring" information flows
DP Personnel and Technology	Specialization for technological learning	User-oriented programmers	Middle management	Establish computer utility and user account teams	Data administration	Data Resource Management
DP Planning and Controls	Lax	More lax	Formalized planning and control	Tailored planning and control systems	Shared data and common systems	Data Resource strategic planning
User Awareness	"Hands off"	Superficially enthusiastic	Arbitrarily held accountable	Accountability learning	Effectively accountable	Acceptance of joint user and data processing accountability
	Stage I Initiation	Stage II Contagion	Stage III Control	Stage IV Integration	Stage V Data Administration	Stage VI Maturity

Level of DP expenditures

Transition point

Source: Richard L. Nolan, "Managing the Crisis in Data Processing," _Harvard Business Review_, March-April 1979. Copyright 1979 by the President and Fellows of Harvard College; all rights reserved. Reprinted by permission of the _Harvard Business Review._

Nolan's work suggests that the researcher can view this evolutionary process by focusing on the changes that occur in the following four variables: technology, portfolio of technology use, organizational structure, and control.

Lodahl (1980) and Zisman (1978) looked more specifically at the introduction of word processing systems in two organizations. Their evidence supports the notion that the application of office automation technologies requires an evolutionary process that brings about shifts in how the technology is used and how the organization is structured. In addition, Lodahl noted that organizations tend to shift the criteria used for purchasing word processing systems as they gain experience with the technology.

Initially, companies invest in word processing equipment believing that they can eliminate some clerical positions. As the organization learns to use the technology, focus shifts to improving managerial effectiveness through the use of expanded word processing capabilities. The cost/benefit criteria shift from "cost avoidance" to "value added."

In this study the author observed the implementation of word processing technology by focusing on the changes in the following four variables: technology, portfolio of technology use, organizational structure, and purchase decision criteria.

A research design was chosen for its ability to enrich our understanding of how organizations purchase and utilize word processing technology, and how the implementation process evolves within different settings over time. A case study approach was chosen as a first step because it provides the best opportunity for gathering detailed information on a company's experience and operations.

The cases were chosen as research sites because they represented companies in different hypothesized stages of the evolution toward implementation success. The goal of the case research was to gather detailed information on the organizational implementation of word processing technology as it occurred over time.

The author studied three organizations — Williamsburg Clothiers (early-transitional user) (disguised name), Corning Glass Works (traditional user), and Lincoln National Life Insurance Company (mature user) — through personal interviews with company executives, reading company documents concerning word processing, and discussions with each company's supplier of word processing equipment. (Appendix A shows the discussion agenda followed for the interviews.)

Williamsburg was classified as an "early" user because it applied word processing technology primarily to the mechanization of typing tasks. Its goal was to improve secretarial productivity and paper output. There was no real attempt made to support managerial activity, or to initiate some kind of work restructuring designed to improve overall productivity. Williamsburg also made no attempt to integrate the technological capabilities of word, data processing, and telecommunications.

Corning, on the other hand, was a more mature user, and therefore closer to implementation success as we have defined it, because they saw the use of word processing as a means of bringing about more effective delegation of work that ultimately would bring about higher payoffs in managerial productivity. The fact that this delegation was not widespread throughout the company, and that Corning, like Williamsburg, had not moved to integrate technologies, makes it "less mature" than the third company studied, Lincoln Life.

At Lincoln, word processing was incorporated into an automated office system designed to increase productivity at all levels of the corporation. Lincoln was the most mature user that the author observed and the most successful, because it was able to use the technology to support a fundamental restructuring of work. Early indications are that the payoff will be substantial. Staff size remained at 1979 levels while sales volume between 1979 and 1981 increased 20 to 25 percent.

Information gathered through these case studies was used as the foundation for a survey questionnaire of 30 companies who belong to the Office Technology Research Group. (See Appendix B for questionnaire.) These companies are not a random sample of word processing users, but rather represent an elite group of companies that have substantial experience with word processing equipment and have committed corporate resources to studying various office automation techniques. As such it was felt that their experience with the technology would provide valuable input to a hypothesis concerned with how the use of word processing technology evolves over time. The companies are from ten different industry groups in the United States, Canada, and Great Britain and range in size from about $300 million in sales to $3 billion.

The cases were used to capture the detail and richness of an organization's experience with the technology, while the questionnaires were used to help ensure that the interpretation of the case data was objective and that the particular cases chosen were not representative. The survey methodology provides a vehicle for looking at the long-term experiences of companies from a cross-section of industries, and therefore it is an important part of a research project designed to examine the process of technology implementation and to generate some hypotheses about it.

4
INDUSTRY ANALYSIS:
THE SUPPLIERS, 1964–79

The purpose of this chapter is to provide the reader with an overview of the word processing industry as a background for examining the evolutionary stage of the product and the competitive nature of the market. To do this we examined the office environment and the technologies that have historically shaped it, as well as the technological and competitive forces that have brought about an explosion in information.

This chapter traces the development of word processing technology and the growth of a new industry designed to address the burgeoning information needs of society in general and business oganizations in particular. To gain some perspective on this issue, consider that by 1950 man had developed as much new information in 50 years as was developed in the previous 3 million years. By 1975 that amount had doubled again.

One solution that emerged to the problem of processing and storing massive amounts of information was the development of computers, which itself accelerated the expansion of knowledge, so that information processing is now one of the major industries of the world, likely to surpass even autos and energy in this decade (IDC).

Much of the information presented in this chapter on product and market development, sales volume, and market shares has been obtained from International Data Corporation and Dataquest, Inc., leading research firms in the field of information processing. The author gratefully acknowledges their assistance and cooperation in preparing this chapter.

While rapid technological growth has taken place in the last 50 years, applications have only recently begun to reach the office. Despite phenomenal productivity gains in all areas of business, a secretary is still able to get only 60 words per minute (WPM) from a typewriter nearly 100 years after its invention. At the same time that industrial productivity has increased almost 90 percent, office productivity has managed only a 4 percent gain, while the cost of operating an office during this period has doubled.

In order to fully understand how word processing evolved and the problems that it solves, we must begin with a historical perspective on information processing and the office environment.

HISTORICAL PERSPECTIVE: THE TYPEWRITER AND BEFORE

Before the nineteenth century and the blossoming of the Industrial Revolution, very few businesses required the services of a full-time administrator (Chandler 1962). The two or three people, usually men and all members of the same family, responsible for the enterprise handled all its basic activities -- economic, administrative, operational, and entrepreneurial.

Administrative activities fell into two broad categories: correspondence and accounting. The basic elements of the correspondence function were the same for those enterprises as they are today for modern multidivisional corporations.

This "correspondence" or "word processing" function can be thought of as a process of taking a thought or idea created in a person's mind, producing a written or hard copy version of that idea, transmitting it to someone else, and storing it or its facsimile for future reference. The four basic elements of this process are as old as civilization itself and are depicted in Figure 4.1.

FIGURE 4.1
Simple Correspondence Function

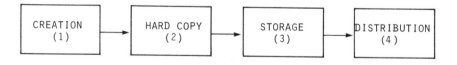

Once ancient people learned to create symbols for their ideas, whether in simple picture form or in alphabetic symbols, they had mastered the first two parts of the process. Earliest writing requirements were probably satisfied by finger drawings in the sand. However, once people desired to store written ideas and distribute them, new technologies were required.

Historians usually date the introduction of writing implements and clay tablets at roughly 4000 B.C. (Hunter 1943). Papermaking can be traced to about 105 A.D. when T'sai Lin, an official attached to the Chinese court, created a sheet of paper using mulberry, fish nets, and hemp waste. Papermaking finally reached Europe in about the tenth century (Hunter). Storing and distributing information had begun long before the introduction of paper, though this invention certainly made it easier.

As early as 1000 B.C. a cylinder mounted on a frame and rolled by hand over a slab of clay became an early duplicating process. Later damp tissue applied against a gum-based ink served the function of duplicating information so that it could be stored or distributed (Hunter).

The need to store and retrieve information, whether from earthenware jars or steel file cabinets, gave rise to the development of filing systems based on alphabetical or chronological ordering.

Distributing information became the next challenge to human technological ingenuity. The invention of the printing press in the 1450s brought about widespread distribution of information (Bell 1979), which allowed for mass education and a dramatic increase in literacy.

The oldest method of getting information across great distances was the messenger. The soldier who ran from Marathon to Athens announcing that the Greeks had defeated the Persians is probably the most famous of these early long-distance communications specialists.

More exotic methods were sometimes employed to get information quickly from distant places. For example, one supposed foundation of the Rothschild fortune was advance information by carrier pigeon of the defeat of Napoleon at Waterloo, so that the Rothschilds could make opportune stock-market decisions (Bell). The oldest established infrastructure for distributing information is the postal service, with historical references to its existence in Egypt in about 2000 B.C.

After the Middle Ages, even with significant advances in printing and distribution and gradual industrialization, most enterprises from ancient times until the mid-nineteenth century remained small single-function organizations. One manager alone, or with the aid of a clerk, handled all of the word processing and other requirements of the business. This pattern was changed dramatically and irrevocably with the coming of the Industrial Revolution. As both Western Europe and the United States began the passage from agrarian to industrial economies, new administrative structures were required to manage the new methods of production.

Factory production, based on the concept of economies of scale, meant that more workers and capital were concentrated in one location, requiring greater administrative ability to coordinate activities. The need to link this production process with the acquiring of raw materials and the eventual marketing of goods brought about the integrated corporate enterprise (Chandler 1962).

The emerging corporate enterprise required for its life and growth vastly more paper work than any number of old-time clerks could efficiently handle. For the first time, attention was given to "managing" or "administering" the word processing function. One technological innovation that revolutionized this process was the typewriter (Current 1954). Attempts at typewriter invention had begun as early as 1700, although invention of the first practical typewriter is usually attributed to the American inventor, Christopher Sholes, in 1867. The factory-based manufacturing process made possible the mass production of precision components, which was a prerequisite to the widespread use of such machinery as the typewriter (Current).

For the businessman trying to handle the increasing complexity brought about by industrialization, the typewriter arrived just in the nick of time. As the Penman's Art Journal observed in 1887, "Five years ago the typewriter was simply a mechanical curiosity, today its monotonous click can be heard in almost every well regulated business in the country. A great revolution is taking place, and the typewriter is at the bottom of it" (Current). The Milwaukee Evening Wisconsin declared in that same year: "Typewriting is as great an improvement on long-hand writing, as steam locomotion is upon the Stage Coach" (Current). The revolution that the typewriter brought about profoundly changed two aspects of modern business: the methods that were used for handling the correspondence function, and the organizational structure of business enterprises.

Before the invention of the typewriter, most businessmen wrote their own letters in longhand in pen and ink. Although office boys and clerks were employed to run errands, pick up and deliver mail, or neatly copy letters or accounting information in longhand, most managers handled all their own correspondence (see Figure 4.2).

FIGURE 4.2
Correspondence Function, before the Typewriter

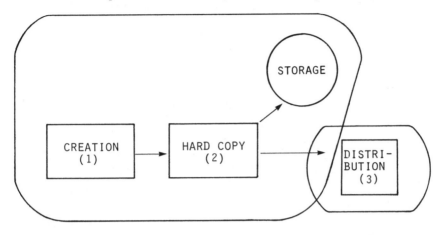

MANAGER   OFFICE BOYS

In terms of the four basic elements of the word processing function, the manager assumed responsibility for creating the document, producing a written version in longhand, and storing a copy of it in a pigeonhole or drawer of a roll-top desk. Office boys assumed responsibility for making copies of originals (by wetting them with felt cloths and then pressing the damp letters against the pages of a book) and making trips to the Post Office to pick up and deliver letters.

With the introduction of the typewriter, a new office worker, the secretary, entered the organizational structure and the correspondence function became a more segmented process, with the secretary assuming responsibility for producing a hard copy and storing it (see Figure 4.3). As one merchant in 1887 observed, "The art of dictation is almost a new art, but it is spreading rapidly and businessmen are beginning to understand that much of their lives had been wasted in the mere mechanical drudgery of letter writing" (Bliven 1954).

The widespread use of the typewriter brought about other advances in office machinery such as the Edison-invented duplicating machine and carbon paper, which when coated on both sides meant that as many as 30 copies could be produced at once.

The ready multiplication of documents saved time and labor, but it also added to labor and wasted time. As early as 1885 a judge complained that typewritten papers were clogging the courts. Formerly, when attorneys themselves wrote what they had to submit, they were mercifully brief, he said. Now that they could dictate to a typist, they were much wordier than they needed to be, and the poor judge found it harder and harder to keep up with his docket (Current).

FIGURE 4.3
Correspondence Function, after the Typewriter

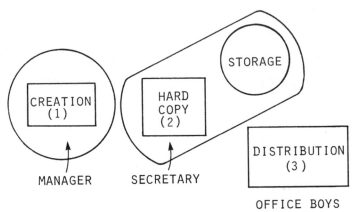

The typewriter, as a technological innovation, became a necessary tool for handling the increasing paper work that was brought about as organizations became increasingly large and complex.

It should not go unmentioned here that another equally dramatic revolution that the typewriter brought about was in bringing large numbers of women into the previously male-only business environment.

Although modern-day feminists view the typewriter as a symbol of holding women to low-paying, low-status jobs, its invention and use provided access to white-collar jobs and reasonable wages for millions of women. It is ironic, in light of the current feminist view toward clerical jobs, that Christopher Sholes, the inventor of the typewriter and an early supporter of women's suffrage, thought that he would probably be best remembered for "having provided an obvious blessing to womenkind" (Current).

With women taking over secretarial positions in large numbers came the advent of the so-called social office and the private secretary tradition (Anderson & Trotter 1974). Private secretaries were hired as administrative "generalists" to provide a variety of support services for managers. In addition to typing, secretaries usually assumed the responsibility for storing information, sorting mail, answering the telephone, and a whole array of other support services. The typical secretary provided this broad range of services for one or two individuals. The private secretary tradition has remained intact since the introduction of the typewriter and the mass entrance of women into secretarial positions.

The typical business office of 1900 with a secretary in starched white blouse answering the phone, typing letters, and scheduling appointments for "the boss" clearly resembles the office of 1970 in terms of job structure and technology. But just as the forces and requirements of the Industrial Revolution brought about a massive change in the operation of nineteenth-century businesses, so the current information explosion and "Communications Revolution" has the potential for bringing about an equally dramatic change in business operations.

The office structure has resisted change for so long partly because both the executive and the secretary opposed new methods and new structures, and partly because radically new technologies have not been available since the typewriter. The office environment that had remained fairly stable for almost a century since the introduction of the typewriter is now undergoing a radical change, in terms of both the technology employed and the structure of the work organization.

Two major events underlie this change: First, management began to take a serious look at the soaring overhead costs of its office operations. An average increase in office costs from 20-30 percent of total company costs to 40-50 percent of total costs represents a significant impact on profitability (Business Week, June 1975). The secretary's job in particular was found to be one of the most poorly designed of any in the office — a random and undermanaged series of typing and nontyping tasks often boring to the secretary and highly wasteful to the firm; the waste is magnified by the fact that the job of secretary is by far the largest single job category in the office.

Second, a new technology, the automatic text-editing typewriter, came onto the market in the late 1960s. This machine "captured" keystrokes by recording text into an electronic memory. This meant that you could then retrieve the stored information and have the machine automatically type out letters or other documents over and over again. You could also easily correct errors or change wording in the recorded text by means of certain editing controls on the keyboard. You did not have to retype a whole long document just because of a few alterations. All the "good" parts of the document remained on the tape; only the portions in need of change were rerecorded. While system capability varies, all machines perform the same functions of input, storage, editing and manipulation, and output.

The text-editing machine allows for almost limitless revision to take place with ease between the idea generation stage and the production of a hard copy. This represents a significant advance and allows for greater flexibility in text composition than has ever been possible with any previous technology for producing hard copy. The use of the high-speed printer means that written text can be produced many times faster than was possible on the typewriter (Kleinschrod 1979).

FIGURE 4.4
Correspondence Function
(Word Processing Technology)
Using a Centralized Group of Operators

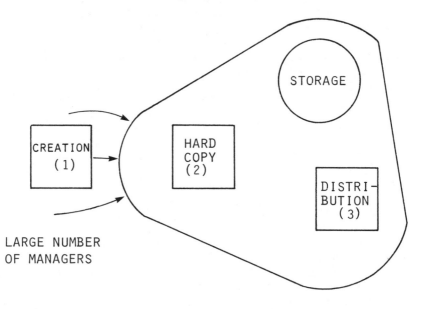

STORAGE

CREATION
(1)

HARD
COPY
(2)

DISTRI-
BUTION
(3)

LARGE NUMBER
OF MANAGERS

TEXT EDITING
EQUIPMENT OPER.

This represents the first truly major technological advance to be introduced into the general office setting since the type-writer (see Figure 4.4). The technological potential of the equipment opens up a broad array of possibilities for reshaping both the content of office work and the organizational structure of businesses in general. To gain a greater appreciation of the technology's potential for change, the following sections will trace the history of the development of the text-editing machine, the growth of product lines, and the exploding sales volume. Finally, we will examine what are likely to be future trends in the industry and discuss what implications this has for competing firms.

WORD PROCESSING: A HISTORY OF
TECHNOLOGY AND PRODUCT DEVELOPMENT

Although something of a mongrel in terms of parentage, the origins of word processing are usually traced to the IBM Magnetic Tape Selectric Typewriter (MT/ST). Word processing as a marketing concept was developed by Ulrich Steinhilter, an IBM office products country manager in Germany, in 1964. He introduced the idea of textverarbeitung shortly after IBM brought out the MT/ST in the European market (Frost and Sullivan 1975). The MT/ST used magnetic tape to store input and was viewed as an improvement over the then available paper tape Frieden Flexowriter automated typewriter. The major markets for these machines were publishing companies and newspapers. They competed for the "low end" of the photo composition market.

Steinhilter, however, conceived of a much broader range of applications for the new machine. He reasoned that since the MT/ST would produce error-free documents once the input was correctly keyboarded, then a substantial increase in office productivity could be achieved if dictation could be directed toward a central transcribing location. Steinhilter sold the MT/ST along with the idea of reorganizing the office. He was successful in persuading IBM USA to go along with his idea, and within a year IBM marketing in the United States had translated the German word into "word processing."

Initially designed as an advanced version of earlier automatic typewriters, the MT/ST's ability to accomplish more than simple automatic letter writing was not immediately realized even by IBM. The system had no buffer memory although it did offer a backspace, strike-over feature. It was not until the subsequent introduction of a dual tape model with the ability to handle large insertions and other revision tasks that true word processing was born. Until production was discontinued in 1972, over 50,000 MT/STs had been installed (IDC).

With the market acceptance of the MT/ST a new approach to office structure and organization was created. The new concept of office structure was predicated on a clear separation of clerical tasks into two distinct categories: word processing and administrative support.

Word Processing	Administrative Support
Dictation	Reception
Copying	Filing
Typing	Mail
	Telephone
	Bookkeeping
	Appointment scheduling
	Office maintenance
	Research
	General service

TABLE 4.1
The Technological Evolution of Word Processing Systems

	1964-71	1972	1973	1974	1975	1976
Innovation	Magnetic Tape/Selectric Typewriter (MT/ST)	MOS* Logic Chips replacing cards and tape as memory device. Visual display on CRT.	Floppy disc storage. High speed, good quality printer	Full page and continuous paging display	Microprocessor-based, programmable word processor	Merging text and data processing capabilities.
Source	IBM	Wang CPT Redactron Lexitron	Vydec Diablo (Xerox)	Lexitron	NBI	DEC Wang
Capabilities	Magnetic tape, no display. Change possible but no insertion possible without erasing the tape. Top quality selectric printed output.	Lower cost chips. Display cards and visual display made ease of operation a major selling point.	Greater storage capacity. Random access discs made retrieval much easier.	Full page display capability was aimed at providing a broad product line, which could meet the needs of a variety of users.	Modular design made upgrading easy. Opened the way for multi-functional workstations.	Localized word and data processing capability opened the potential of "word processing" to perform a variety of office tasks such as billing and statistics as well as text.
Uses/Users	Form letters. Typing pools — required a lot of training.	Replacing low end of print market. Easier operation broadened its appeal to typists. Broader based typing market — not just repetitive typing but also when there were a lot of revisions.	Lower cost, ease of operation word processing equipment a likely choice for typewriter replacement.		Marketing emphasis now is on the broader task of managing information. Potential market is business or professional enterprise.	

*metal oxide silicon

With the workload divided, it now became possible for one administrative secretary and one word processing secretary to produce the same amount of work that had previously required three general secretaries doing both kinds of tasks. The MT/ST was the pioneer product in word processing that sparked the development of a legion of new products and companies over the next 15 years (see Table 4.1).

Using the design of the MT/ST as a basis, IBM next introduced a system that would automatically generate typewriter material with a justified right margin instead of the ragged margins produced by a conventional typewriter. The MT/ST enabled users to produce in-house, camera-ready copy suitable for high-quality applications such as brochures, manuals, and promotional material.

After the MT/ST had been on the market for a few years, IBM saw that it was not a universal system for all organizations. As early as 1975 IBM was forced to back off from its rigid view that the secretarial job should be abolished. As William Loughlin, vice president of IBM's Office Products Division acknowledged, centralization was good for certain operations and applications, but proved disastrous as a universal concept (Business Week, June 1975). The MT/ST and reorganization of the office did nothing to meet the needs of low-volume users with light revision requirements.

In 1969 IBM introduced the first of its magnetic card devices, the MagCard I. The storage medium employed was a simple magnetic card, in contrast to the reel-to-reel magnetic tape of MT/ST. The card-to-page relationship was popular with operators because it was easier to understand and use than the more complicated tape storage of the MT/ST. The MagCard I, however, offered little new to solve the many other problems of typing.

IBM addressed the communications problem by attaching an acoustic coupler to MagCard I. This enabled a user to transmit or receive text instantly via the telephone lines. Word processing could now add instant relay to its growing list of capabilities. The Executive MagCard offered the additional capability of proportionately spaced type, a more professional-looking copy where an "m" takes up more room than an "i," for a better appearance.

Up to this point, IBM had been the leading force in word processing. It was its technology and its products that dominated the market. IBM had accomplished all this in fact without offering a system with a buffer memory. When the MagCard II was introduced in 1973, with its 800-character memory, a slowly and steadily growing market was transformed into one of the glamour industries of the decade. The buffer memory permitted nearly unlimited revision capability. Large insertions, automatic centering, automatic decimal alignment, automatic underscoring, switching and merging of mail lists could be accomplished with heretofore unheard of ease. It was compatible with other MagCard models and its price was roughly equivalent to the MT/ST.

The MagCard II offered solutions to the basic problems of typing and, with the power of IBM behind it, established the market for text-editing typing systems. As demand for text-editing machines grew rapidly, other companies began to enter the field. In 1972 Xerox Corporation purchased Diablo systems from Itel Corporation to acquire the 30-character-per-second printer that Diablo had developed. To enter the word processing market, Xerox wanted something innovative. This new single-element printing device with few moving parts, electronic, 30-character-per-second speed (versus 15 for an IBM Selectric) appeared to give Xerox the opportunity it was looking for. Xerox initially offered the printer to original equipment manufacturers (OEMs) for use with computer terminals. In October 1974 Xerox brought out the Model 800 Word Processor, offering the product in dual card or cassette versions (Frost and Sullivan 1975).

Several companies in the late 1960s worked at developing text-editing systems that would employ a cathode ray tube (CRT) to display text on a screen rather than typing directly onto paper. The first company to successfully market such a product was Lexitron corporation (IDC). Text that was being typed as well as that which had been previously recorded was displayed on the screen. The operator made all revisions on the screen, then stored the text on a magnetic medium or played it out on an off-line printer. The printer was separate, which made simultaneous input and output a major selling point of display screen systems. Lexitron used magnetic tape cassettes for text storage and offered a choice of either an IBM executive printer or the faster Diablo.

Vydec, Inc., an affiliate of Exxon, introduced in 1973 a display screen system with one important advantage over the Lexitron system. The Vydec editor was the first word processing system to offer the flexible or "floppy" diskette as its storage medium. Because of its ability to permit random rather than sequential access to stored text, and its greater storage capacity and its lower cost per stored page, the floppy diskette became the standard medium for most CRT stand-alone systems. Both Lexitron and Vydec systems offered a "full-page" screen display, as many as 66 lines of text (IDC).

The development of relatively inexpensive minicomputers in the mid-1970s led several companies including LCS (a pioneer in the field -- now defunct) and Wang to develop text-editing systems utilizing the power of data processing. Typing stations with screens and keyboards, but little or no revision logic, were connected to a central processing unit, which allowed the sharing of a large storage base as well as the sophisticated editing software of the minicomputers. Printers were also shared, normally two or three typing stations to one printer. Most display screen stand-alone systems could compete in smaller installations, but where four or five typing stations were required, shared logic systems began to show a lower per-station cost.

In 1975, NBI, a small Colorado-based firm, first introduced microprocessor technology to word processing. This innovation meant that NBI's machines were programmable and could either function as stand-alones or in clusters. This design approach made future upgrading of equipment very easy. By the late 1970s the microprocessor-based modular design became the standard for the industry.

In 1970 the term "word processing" was synonymous with IBM. In 1980 more than 50 companies manufactured or distributed text-editing systems. In addition to this increase in the number of manufacturers, the number and variety of products available has also increased dramatically.

PRODUCT LINES

Under the general heading of "word processing," seven distinct product groups have emerged: electronic typewriters, stand-alone nondisplay units, single-line or "thin window" display units, stand-alone display units, clustered or shared resource systems, hybrid systems, and time sharing. Although all products share the characteristics of being electronically based, providing for storing, editing, and reproduction of text, there are substantial differences in price and capability between product groups. While all equipment manufacturers claim to bring the customer into the "office of the future," the products themselves have different capabilities and are sold to different market segments.

Electronic Typewriters

Electronic typewriters fill the gap between ordinary type-writers and the more expensive display-oriented word processing equipment. All electronic typewriters share at least seven traits. They all look like typewriters and lack a video display screen. All incorporate microcircuits, a fixed carriage, and a typing mechanism that moves across the page as it prints. Their memory capacity makes it easier to correct mistakes, since most electronic typewriters remember an entire line of what has been typed and will automatically wipe it out if instructed to do so.

Compared to word processors with video terminals that cost $7,500 and up, electronic typewriters are inexpensive. They vary from $895 to over $8,000 for an elaborate version of Exxon's Qyx. At an average price of $2,000 the most popular machines can store several pages of text and automate most repetitive everyday typing tasks like signature blocks or addresses. Most can be programmed to do centering, columns, or to hop from blank to blank on purchase-order forms so that a secretary need only fill in the missing information (see Fortune, December 29, 1980). IBM, Exxon, and Olivetti are the major competitors in this end of the market.

Despite the current fascination with merging word and data processing functions into sophisticated multifunction terminals, industry observers expect that the electronic typewriters will continue to enjoy rising popularity well into the next decade, especially in small offices.

Stand-Alone Nondisplay Units

These machines were among the first word processors sold and include the original IBM MagCard machines, which will not be sold after 1981. According to estimates by Dataquest, the 20-year span from 1963 to 1983 encompasses the complete rise and fall of this type of word processing machine. Displaced by CRT-based units, demand for nondisplay units should continue to decline and eventually phase out by 1984.

Single-Line or "Thin Window" Display Units

These machines allow the operator to view text one line at a time through a small screen. The first of these units appeared in the mid-1970s. Priced below the display units, sales of these products have enjoyed a modest growth and Dataquest estimates that these products should retain their roughly 20 percent share of the total word processing market.

Stand-Alone Display Units

These machines include a keyboard, separate printer, and video screen. The editing is performed on the screen and the memory is usually floppy disc. This segment of the market reached its landmark for growth in 1976, and so far it has been the fastest-growing segment. On a cumulative basis, Dataquest estimates that approximately 146,000 units will be installed by 1980 and the number should rise to 927,000 by 1984. The overwhelming popularity of the display screen versus nondisplay or printer-based systems makes this particular product the standard for the industry.

Clustered or Shared Resource Systems

Clustered systems are multiterminal units that attach to a central processing unit (CPU) to handle communications and maintain a separate document base. International Data Corporation estimates that this will be the fastest-growing segment of the word processing market in the next decade (see Figures 4.5 and 4.6). Part of the appeal of this product is that the cost per terminal is cheaper than stand-alone systems if the customer buys more than four or five terminals. Also, the CPU allows for central storage of information and, therefore, remote access from different terminals. This is different from stand-alone systems where information is usually physically contained on a disc at the work station. Wang has been the leader in this particular segment of the market, although its rapid growth rate has enticed other competitors into the market.

FIGURE 4.5
U.S. Word Processing Shipments,
IDC Estimates of Product Mix, 1978-84

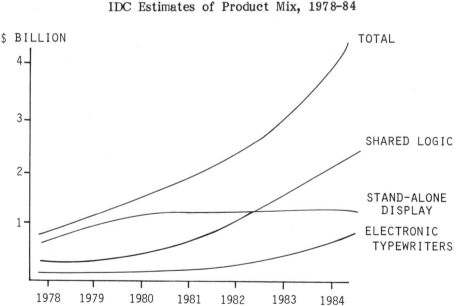

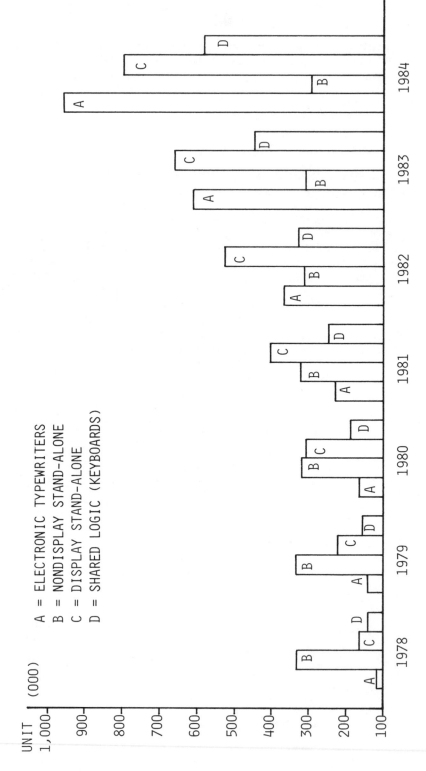

FIGURE 4.6

Word Processing Units Installed in the United States, 1978-84

A = ELECTRONIC TYPEWRITERS
B = NONDISPLAY STAND-ALONE
C = DISPLAY STAND-ALONE
D = SHARED LOGIC (KEYBOARDS)

Hybrid Systems

This category usually includes display units combining data and word processing capability. They are also referred to as "multifunction work stations." Some of the characteristics of these work stations include the ability to:

- Move information between text and data files easily.
- Run small business applications such as billing, accounts receivable, or inventory control.
- Support a wide range of easy-to-use graphics.
- Support advanced office functions such as electronic mail and calendar management.

Not surprisingly, the leaders in this segment of the market have been the computer mainframe manufacturers — such as Wang, Prime, DEC, and, to some extent, IBM — who have pushed the fully integrated approach to office automation.

Time Sharing

This refers to purchasing the text-editing power of a CPU through a dumb terminal on a pay-as-you-go basis. In the early 1970s this was a popular approach and Bowne Time Sharing Inc., a subsidiary of Bowne & Co., the oldest and one of the largest financial printers in the country, was the major supplier of computerized text-editing services (Frost and Sullivan). However, with the declining cost of word processing hardware, it appears that the time-sharing approach is likely to phase out.

MARKET DEVELOPMENT

The demand for traditional typewriters grew out of a need for greater correspondence productivity, that is, a greater speed of putting words on paper, as well as the need to create acceptable-looking hard copy.

The initial development of word processing equipment appears to have been a logical extension of conventional typewriters using technologies borrowed from data processing equipment as well as some created by the word processing companies themselves. The early applications of word processing technology were aimed at automating the more repetitive aspects of the typing function. For example, such applications as "customized form" letters or rapid preparation of semicustom letters or reports using standard paragraphs were among the first uses of word processing equipment.

As we have seen, IBM was the pioneer in this field, first with its MT/ST and later its MagCard machines. Both of those machines were sold through IBM's Office Products Division and were marketed as automated typewriters. While IBM did attempt to sell an office automation concept — that is, splitting the secretarial functions in half with typing done in a central location and administrative support provided locally by other secretaries — the company's emphasis was on improving productivity through improving the secretarial function.

During the early and mid-1970s IBM did not emphasize, at least in its word processing effort, the integration of various computer-based systems for both managers and secretaries. At the same time during the mid-1970s, several new companies were coming into the market — some on the strength of their technological expertise, such as NBI, Vydec, Wang, and others, such as Lanier, seeking to expand an already established base in the office products market.

IBM, the market leader, was slow to pick up on such innovations as the CRT display screen and the floppy disc, largely because of its policy not to obsolesce its rather large installed base of MagCard machines. In the meantime the demand for word processing systems continued to grow rapidly, paced by:

- Traditional demand resulting from the need to create typed documents.
- Derived demand, generated by the availability of new products that permitted other functions to be performed (Dataquest, Inc. information) (see Table 4.2).

IBM held its own at the low end of the market with electronic typewriters and MagCard machines but was not a major force in the fast-growing stand-alone display or clustered systems segments of the market. Consequently, its share of the total market declined dramatically between 1972 and 1980 (see Table 4.3 and Figure 4.7).

To gain a better understanding of how these dramatic shifts in technology and market share have occurred, we examined some of the major competitors in the industry and their strategies.

COMPETITORS AND COMPETITIVE STRATEGIES

The enormous growth rate in sales and the relatively easy access to word processing technology has enticed a number of companies to enter this booming market. Table 4.4 shows most of the major competing firms in 1980 and the breadth of products that each offers. For companies such as Wang, DEC,

TABLE 4.2

Work Station Market Forecast Summary in Dollars, 1974-84
(in thousands [K] or millions [M] of dollars or units)

Region/Country: U.S.
Company: All

Model: All
Segment: All

	1974	1975	1976	1977	1978	1979	1980	1981	1982	1983	1984
Deliveries (K)	32.9	37.6	45.3	50.5	67.6	94.6	136.3	209.2	285.0	371.2	466.1
Cumulative deliveries (K)	130.9	168.5	213.8	264.3	331.9	426.3	562.8	772.0	1,057.0	1,428.2	1,894.3
Units in use (K)	124.9	158.6	200.0	246.5	310.2	400.9	533.3	738.6	1,019.6	1,386.9	1,849.1
Units sold direct (K)	9.0	6.9	9.0	10.2	20.7	43.3	67.4	99.8	132.7	174.2	228.3
Sold to dealers (K)	1.4	3.6	4.6	3.6	5.3	9.0	16.1	21.0	26.9	35.1	39.0
Subtotal (K)	10.4	10.5	13.6	13.8	26.0	52.3	83.5	120.8	159.6	209.3	267.3
Rent converts (K)	5.4	8.8	10.4	12.0	16.4	19.9	24.8	28.1	31.6	34.4	48.1
Total sold (K)	15.8	19.3	24.0	25.8	42.4	72.2	108.3	148.9	191.2	243.7	315.4
Cumulative sold (K)	33.0	52.3	76.3	102.1	144.5	216.7	325.0	473.9	665.1	908.8	1,224.2
Direct sale price ($K)	6.1	7.0	7.8	9.0	9.1	8.4	7.7	7.5	7.3	6.8	6.6
Dealer sale price ($K)	5.1	4.3	4.8	5.6	6.3	6.3	5.6	5.4	5.0	4.3	4.1
Direct sale revenue ($M)	54.9	48.3	70.6	91.5	187.9	362.4	519.0	748.8	973.9	1,187.6	1,500.6
Dealer sale revenue ($M)	7.2	15.5	22.0	20.2	33.6	56.3	90.5	112.9	133.9	150.4	161.2
Rent convert revenue ($M)	30.9	43.6	52.4	60.4	84.8	99.6	88.4	94.8	110.5	121.9	174.4
Total sales revenue ($M)	93.0	107.4	145.0	172.0	306.4	518.3	697.9	956.6	1,218.3	1,459.9	1,836.2
If sold value ($M)	302.1	353.3	429.2	518.5	706.5	899.7	1,161.9	1,728.4	2,242.6	2,683.0	3,247.1
Average sale price ($K)	5.9	5.6	6.0	6.7	7.2	7.2	6.4	6.4	6.4	6.0	5.8
New units rented (K)	22.5	27.1	31.7	36.7	41.6	42.3	52.8	88.4	125.4	161.9	198.8
Year end rental population (K)	99.8	118.1	139.4	164.1	189.3	211.7	239.7	300.0	393.8	521.3	672.0
Average rental population (K)	94.0	108.9	128.8	151.8	176.7	200.5	225.7	269.9	346.9	457.6	596.7
Annual unit rent revenue ($K)	2.9	2.9	3.0	3.2	3.4	3.4	3.5	3.7	3.7	3.7	3.6
Total rent revenues ($M)	270.8	314.7	387.6	479.1	595.5	682.1	799.0	995.0	1,288.3	1,671.2	2,132.3
Total workstation revenue ($M)	363.8	422.1	532.6	651.1	901.9	1,200.4	1,496.9	1,951.6	2,506.7	3,131.2	3,968.5

Source: Dataquest, Inc., estimates, October 10, 1980.

51

TABLE 4.3

Work Station Market Forecast in Units, 1972-83

Region/Country: U.S. Display Segment: All
Company: All Config. Segment: All
Model: All, by company Status: All

Deliveries, Share in Percent

	1972	1973	1974	1975	1976	1977	1978	1979	1980	1981	1982	1983
AM International	—	—	—	—	—	.6	2.2	2.5	2.4	2.3	2.4	1.8
Artec	—	—	—	—	.2	.8	.9	1.0	1.5	1.2	1.0	1.3
Burroughs/Redac	4.9	7.6	6.4	7.4	4.4	3.1	3.9	3.1	3.9	2.0	1.7	1.5
CPT—all	2.5	3.8	3.5	4.5	4.8	5.3	4.8	4.5	2.6	1.8	.9	.3
A.B. Dick—all	—	—	—	—	1.5	5.1	4.8	2.4	5.0	5.2	4.5	4.3
DEC—all	—	—	—	—	.2	1.2	1.7	3.0	1.2	1.3	1.7	2.0
Four Phase	—	—	—	—	—	—	.4	1.0				
IBM (OP+GS+DP)—all	92.8	84.8	75.7	62.2	58.3	53.8	39.2	26.0	20.1	18.6	19.5	21.0
Lanier—all	—	—	—	—	.9	1.8	7.4	8.6	4.7	3.4	2.3	2.0
Ray Lex—all	.6	1.4	2.0	2.9	2.6	2.3	3.5	3.7	3.9	2.9	2.5	1.8
3M—all	—	—	.6	.8	.9	1.0	1.2	.7	.4	.3		
NBI—all	—	—	—	—	—	.2	.6	1.2	1.1	1.2	1.1	.4
NBI—all	—	—	—	—	.2	1.4	1.4	2.1	1.3	1.3	1.1	.5
Olivetti—all	—	—	—	—	.2	.4	3.5	6.3	3.4	2.4	1.4	.8
Olympia—all	—	—	—	—	—	—	—	—	1.5	1.5	1.1	.8
Phil/Micom—all	—	—	—	—	.2	.6	.7	—	2.0	2.5	1.7	1.0
Qyx—all	—	—	—	—	—	—	1.9	9.7	13.8	16.3	17.8	17.6
Sevin—all	—	2.4	10.2	14.6	12.1	2.5	2.2	2.2	.9	.3	.1	—
TI—all	—	—	—	—	—	—	—	—	.9	3.0	5.2	7.5
Triumph/Royal/Adler—all	—	—	—	—	—	—	—	—	1.1	1.3	1.1	.8
Vydec—all	—	—	.9	1.6	2.4	4.9	4.5	2.2	2.8	2.2	2.9	3.0
Wang—all	—	—	—	—	1.1	4.9	7.7	10.3	10.5	10.0	7.4	6.7
Xerox—all	—	—	.6	6.1	9.9	10.2	7.8	9.6	9.6	10.3	11.0	10.1
Other—all	—	—	—	—	—	—	—	—	5.4	8.7	11.4	15.0
Totals	100.0	100.0	100.0	100.0	100.0	100.0	100.0	100.0	100.0	100.0	100.0	100.0

Source: Dataquest, July 19, 1979.

FIGURE 4.7
Total Word Processing Market and
IBM Market Share 1972 and 1980

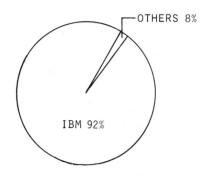

OTHERS 8%

IBM 92%

1972

TOTAL MARKET ～$300 MILLION

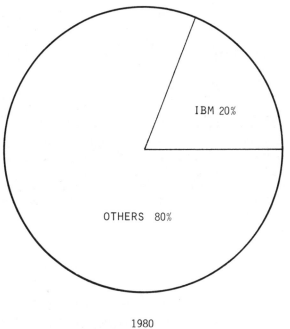

IBM 20%

OTHERS 80%

1980

(ESTIMATED) TOTAL MARKET = $1.5 BILLION

Source: IDC estimates.

Prime, and Datapoint, who have a strong position in the data processing or minicomputer market, their entry into the word processing market can be viewed as an attempt to protect their major product lines by increasing the number of functions, such as word processing, available to their customers. For the most part these companies have emphasized the integrated nature of information management and as such are a major force in the clustered systems as well as the hybrid or multifunction segment of the market. They are newcomers to the traditional office products market, which includes typewriters, dictating equipment, furniture, and stationery supplies.

For companies such as Lanier and Xerox, entry into the word processing market represents an opportunity to expand the number of products they can make available to their traditional customers. Lanier is a leading competitor in the dictation equipment market, while Xerox is of course a major competitor in the copying and duplicating market.

IBM's Office Products Division introduced the initial word processing products that industry observers now estimate will replace traditional typewriter sales by the end of the decade.

For small technology-based companies such as NBI or CPT, the word processing market represented an opportunity to take advantage of rapid sales growth, low barriers to entry, and relatively high margins that were available in the mid-1970s, particularly for innovative firms.

In this section a sample of firms competing in the word processing market, their major product lines, and their competitive strategies will be described. The firms were chosen to provide the reader with an understanding of what the market leaders were doing as well as to present a broad view of the different competitive strategies present in the market.

The information for this section was gathered from both published sources and interviews with key personnel in the vendor firms. The companies examined are IBM, Wang, Lanier, Exxon, NBI, and Prime.

IBM

IBM has been characterized as "the company that essentially created the word processing market only to see it slip away" (Electronics, July 1980). Although it seems unlikely that this giant in the information industry will remain down for long, the cause of its slipping position in the word processing market can be traced to two corporate policies:

● Commitment not to rapidly obsolesce installed IBM equipment.
● Policy not to permit the Office Products Division to sell products with potential data processing capability.

TABLE 4.4
Office Equipment Manufacturers and Depth of Product Line

	IBM	Xerox	3M	Exxon	Raytheon	Burroughs	Olivetti	DEC	Datapoint	AM International	A.B. Dick	Wang	Four Phase	Lanier	CPT	NBI	Micom	Prime
Electronic typewriter	X	X		X			X											
Electric typewriter	X	X					X											
Stand-alone, nondisplay	X	X				X	X		X	X			X	X	X			
Stand-alone, display	X	X	X	X		X	X	X	X	X		X	X	X	X	X	X	
Stand-alone, single line	X	X		X			X	X					X	X	X	X	X	
Clustered systems	X	X	X					X	X	X		X	X	X				
Hybrid systems	X	X	X					X	X	X		X	X	X				X
Copies/duplicators	X	X	X				X			X								
Facsimile	X	X	X	X		X				X								
OCR	X	X				X			X	X								
Micrographics	X	X	X		X				X	X	X							
Photo composition									X	X	X	X						
Graphic printer, NIPS	X	X							X		X	X		X				
Dictation	X			X							X	X						
Electronic mail	X							X	X									
Teleconferencing																		
Computers	X				X	X	X	X	X		X	X	X				X	X
Networking	X	X				X	X	X	X		X	X	X					

55

Within the Office Products Division (OPD) IBM has demonstrated an extraordinary ability to sell, service, and finance new products. Between 1964 and 1972, IBM virtually created the word processing market, convincing the traditional office products market to buy a fairly-difficult-to-operate system (Frost and Sullivan 1975). However, as technological change came into the market, IBM, instead of responding quickly, chose to proceed slowly and not obsolesce its large installed base of MagCard machines. In 1978 International Data Corporation estimated that 65 percent of the total U.S. installed base of stand-alone word processors were IBM MagCard machines.

When IBM did respond with the OS/6, it was offered by the General Systems Division, as was the 5520. Both systems were compatible with MagCard input and output and provided a natural upgrade for IBM's large base of MagCard typewriters.

Because the General Systems Division (GSD) offered both the System 6 and the 5520, neither product was able to gain the full benefit of the OPD's well-trained sales force of over 4,000 representatives in 200 branches. This, coupled with the fact that both systems were considered technologically inferior to what the competitors were offering, spelled disaster for these two products.

IBM then introduced the 3730, an office communications system that was a distributed/clustered word and data processing system that could be operated either as a separate cluster system or connected to a host IBM 370 mainframe computer. The system could support up to 12 display terminals.

The 3730 was a word processing system offered from the Data Processing (DP) rather than the Office Products Division. This was in keeping with IBM's policy not to permit the OPD to sell equipment with data processing capability. However, the DP Division targeted its marketing effort to its traditional data processing customers, offering office automation support through the data processing departments. This proved to be an unsuccessful marketing approach to selling word processing/office automation equipment. For the most part, during the 1970s companies were experimenting with less sophisticated nonintegrated systems, and the buying decisions were being made by nondata processing people.

While IBM wrestled with the organizational question of what division should sell which products, they lost ground rapidly in the fast-growing stand-alone display segment and in the clustered systems segment of the market. IBM remained strongest in the low end of the market with its electronic typewriters. These products were marketed through the traditional sales approach of the OPD. Although Qyx and Olivetti were entering this market with competitive "intelligent typewriters," this segment of the market remains IBM's stronghold in the overall word processing market.

To stem its declining market share, in June 1980, IBM announced a new product and a new product policy. The company unveiled the Displaywriter, a stand-alone, display-based, microprocessor-driven word processor with a price tag of $7,895, the lowest in the industry. The new Displaywriter was designed with a lot of attention to ease of use and operator comfort, an increasingly important design criterion in office systems.

The display screen offers a full 25 lines, the largest offered by IBM, and easy-to-use special function keys and English language prompts to assist the operator. A unique feature is its spelling verification function, which can check the spelling of 50,000 words. In addition, the user can add up to 500 specialized words to the directory. The product will be offered and sold through the Office Products Division.

In a statement of corporate policy made at the same time the Displaywriter was announced, an IBM spokesman said that its three divisions — Office Products, Data Processing, and General Systems — would all continue to offer a broad range of products and refine their offerings to provide a variety of solutions to customer needs.

Chauncey Bartholet, directory of Market Requirements Planning for IBM's Corporate Marketing Department, said that the company plans to provide communications to support the integration of these products into single enterprise-wide solutions. "The Corporation will depend on its three divisions to cooperate in deciding which products are best for a particular customer's problems" (Electronics, July 1980).

IBM's new product and product policy means that the company will now aggressively go after the stand-alone display segment and combine its rather formidable resources to go after the clustered and multifunction segments of the market. Organizationally, IBM will no longer adhere to the product differentiation strategy that originally splintered its marketing thrust, but instead it will seek to mass the capabilities of all of its divisions to solve customer needs.

Making organizational cooperation a reality will probably be the toughest challenge facing IBM in the next decade. However, with net earnings in 1979 in excess of $3 billion, and Office Products the fastest growing segment of IBM's business, the company has the ability and the incentive to pull it off.

Wang

Wang Laboratories was founded in 1951 by Dr. An Wang, whose pioneering work in the field of magnetic core memories was the basis for this high-technology company. The company's original products were electronic calculators that out-performed the then available mechanical machines and were sold principally to the engineering and scientific market.

When the bottom began to fall out of the calculator market in the early 1970s, Wang began developing small computers as well as word processing machines. Wang soon earned a reputation for quality and performance in the minicomputer business, based on healthy investments in R&D and the ability to produce quality products.

Seeing the market potential for word processing as early as 1972, Dr. Wang, who has remained the driving force in the company, set a corporate goal to split revenues evenly between small computer and word processing products. In 1974 word processing products accounted for 12 percent of total revenues, while in 1979 word processing and office information systems accounted for more than 50 percent of the company's revenues.

In developing its minicomputer and word processing products, Wang established the policy that both products must use identical components. This policy meant that Wang was the first company to offer a truly integrated information management system.

During the mid-1970s Wang kept pace with the technological innovations being made in the market and introduced some of its own, including the use of MOS logic chips in its word processing products to improve price/performance ratio.

In 1976 Wang announced three new product lines: the Wang 10, 20, and 30. The 10 was a stand-alone display-based unit and the other two were clustered systems. The Wang 30, the larger of the two cluster systems, used traditional computer hard disc storage, which was the first of its kind in the word processing industry and permitted the greatest amount of information storage. All three of these systems were compatible with each other in terms of operating procedures, protocols, and software.

The result of Dr. Wang's policy of making all components interchangeable meant that Wang products were easily upgradeable. Wang thus pioneered the clustered system and interchangeability concept.

In 1978 Wang announced a new product line called the Office Information System (OIS), which allowed for both word and data processing, looked much more like a minicomputer than the company's other word processing products, and was designed to overcome some of the limitations inherent in even the largest word processing system. For example, the OIS had a sophisticated operating system that allowed for greater file protection and user programming. Wang also began offering a word processing package on its supermini, the VS computer.

Wang's strategy has been to provide a broad line of compatible products that are close to the leading edge of technology and are easily upgradeable. The strategy seems to have paid off handsomely for Wang. Between 1978 and 1979 revenues increased 62 percent from $198 million to $321.6 million. Net earnings increased by 83 percent from $15.6 million to $28.6 million, while the company maintained a healthy return on capital of 19 percent (1979 Annual Report).

In December 1980 the company announced a new product, the Wangwriter, which is a stand-alone display unit positioned to compete head on with IBM's new Displaywriter and the other offerings in this segment of the market. The product is priced equivalently to IBM's new offering and, Wang claims, offers more options and is more easily upgradeable to the company's larger systems when and if the customer is ready. This new product offering is in keeping with Wang's strategy of offering a broad product line so that the user can buy into the Wang system with almost any level of product configuration or complexity. The new Wangwriter will give the company a new product for the low end of the market where it has been weakest and give the company better access to small first-time users.

Wang's competitive strengths are its technical expertise and the easy upgradeability of its products. The company is well positioned to offer both clustered systems and fully integrated multifunction systems, which are projected to be the fastest growing segments in the next decade (see Figure 4.5). Wang has also enjoyed good market acceptance for its products. Its cancellation rates on rentals are among the lowest in the industry (personal interview data).

The principal challenges facing Wang will be to manage the rapid growth the company is experiencing while maintaining product integrity and service support. In 1979 the company's backlog of orders grew by 133 percent to a record $163 million, stretching company personnel in all areas of the business.

In addition the Wang family has continued to maintain a tight control on the business, which so far has not presented any problems. Because of Wang's strong financial performance, the company was able to offer two classes of common stock: Class B shares, which have only one-tenth of a vote; and Class C shares, 54 percent of which are owned by Dr. Wang and his family and have full voting power. Family control goes beyond stock ownership to operating responsibilities. Fred Wang, Dr. Wang's 30-year-old son, is in charge of new product development and son Courtney, 24, is breaking into the business by selling equipment in the Denver area. As the company continues to grow and require more managerial talent as well as capital, Dr. Wang may have to choose between maintaining control and meeting the demands of growth.

Wang's strategy of offering an across-the-board line of products puts it into direct competition with IBM, which is the only other company that offers so complete a product line. The financial resources and marketing prowess of IBM make it a formidable head-to-head competitor. Wang's products are at the moment more easily upgradeable than IBM's and Wang does not have the problem of coordinating the sales effort of different divisions. Currently the Wang sales force is organized so that sales representatives carrying word processing equipment and those carrying minicomputers work out of the same office and report to the same branch manager, which makes coordinating customer needs easier. Wang's original sales expertise was in the engineering and scientific markets, and it is likely to face real competition in the word processing market as more vendors begin offering clustered systems, a product line that Wang has so far dominated.

The broad product line approach also makes the company vulnerable to attack by competitors who target their products to attract specific market segments. Such competition would include Vydec and Lanier. Lanier, in particular, with its aggressive sales force and new line of clustered systems has begun to cut seriously into this segment of the market (see Table 4.5 and Figure 4.8).

TABLE 4.5
U.S. Installed Base of Clustered Systems (1978)

Supplier	Systems	Average Keyboards/ System	Keyboards	Share (keyboards)
Wang	2,000	3.4	6,800	31.9
Four-Phase	650	3.8	2,500	11.7
Xerox	400	5.0	2,000	9.4
Datapoint	350	4.3	1,500	7.0
AM Jacquard	240	5.0	1,200	5.6
DEC	285	4.0	1,150	5.4
General Computer Systems	80	10.0	800	3.8
Wordstream/MAI	150	5.0	750	3.5
Comptek	100	6.0	600	2.8
Edit Systems, Inc.	100	5.0	500	2.4
Others	695	5.0	3,500	16.5
Total	5,050	4.2	21,300	100.0

Source: IDC.

FIGURE 4.8
1979 U.S. Clustered Word Processor Shipments

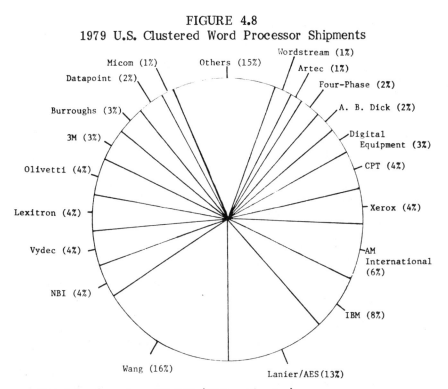

Total keyboards = 85,000 (IDC estimates).

Source: IDC.

Wang has managed consistently to offer high quality, high performance products and undoubtedly will continue to maintain its commitment to product innovation. The major challenge facing Wang will be to maintain product quality and service support in the face of tougher competition and the demands of rapid growth.

Lanier Business Products, Inc.

Lanier was founded in 1934 and operated as a subsidiary of Oxford Industries until July 1977 when it was spun off and became a separate corporation listed on the New York Stock Exchange. The Atlanta-based company is headed by former salesman Gene Milner, son-in-law of the late J. Hicks Lanier, who ran the company in the 1940s. Milner's aggressive style has brought Lanier from a regional distributor of dictating machines with $12 million in sales in 1965 to a nationwide manufacturing and marketing company for dictating and word processing equipment, with sales in 1979 of $183 million (Loving, 1979). The company is also a major distributor of 3M products. Lanier's strategy has been to stress marketing innovations, product development, and an aggressive sales strategy. This policy has paid off in both the dictating equipment and word processing markets.

In the dictation market Dictaphone dominated the field for years, but in 1975 Lanier pushed ahead to gain a 33 percent share of the market and the market lead. This impressive performance was paced by Lanier's innovative product introductions: recording cassettes, like those used in home tape recorders, and the minicassettes, with adapters so that both sizes could be used interchangeably. Lanier also introduced pocket-sized dictation machines.

In 1976, spotting the growing market for word processors, Lanier bought a 36 percent interest in AES Data Ltd. (Automatic Electronic Systems), an ailing Canadian company that had developed a stand-alone unit. AES was originally formed by a group of Montreal entrepreneurs. The president and founder, Steve Dorsey, left when the company was acquired and formed MICOM, which has since been bought out by Philips Electronics (see Seybold Report, October 1979). By 1978 Lanier had taken the market lead in the stand-alone display segment of the market (see Figure 4.9).

The Lanier "No Problem" Word Processor was the product that paced the company's impressive growth. This machine utilized floppy disc storage, an IBM microprocessor, and a display screen. Its market appeal was that it was easy to operate and learn. Lanier has equipped the machine with a so-called special-function key instead of the more complicated codes that early word processors used. For example, if you wanted to delete a line or paragraph, there was on the Lanier machine a button labeled "delete" that you could press instead of some other code to accomplish the same task. In addition to its special-function keys the company provided training as part of the product package. The "No Problem" LC (large capacity) unit was introduced in fiscal 1979, allowing for greater data storage. With both systems customers can select from a series of "Smart Disc" programs that can easily be inserted into the machine to expand its capabilities to meet specific needs. For example, Smart Disc applications include financial, billing, and statistical packages.

Lanier uses a "down home" approach to marketing. In order to broaden the appeal of its products, Lanier's salespeople bring word processing to its lowest common denominator. They refer to their video terminal word processor as an electronic typewriter. They call the division responsible for marketing these products the "typing division" and the person who heads it is called the Vice President in Charge of Typing (Seybold Report).

FIGURE 4.9
U.S. Stand-alone Word Processing Unit Shipments, 1978

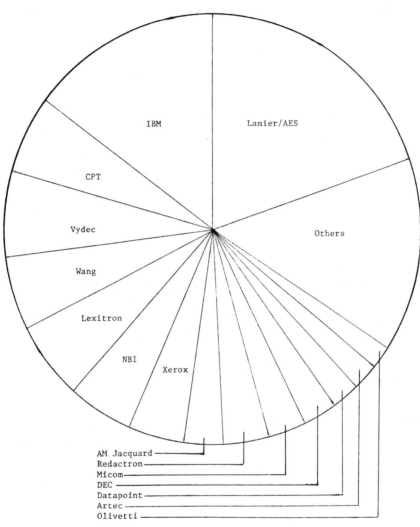

Total units = 41,830.

Source: IDC.

All Lanier sales representatives carry the full line of the company's products: dictating equipment, word processors, and 3M products. The sales pitch is aimed at secretaries and first-line supervisors. Lanier sells simplicity, practicality, and productivity. The company backs away from sophisticated technical talk as it feels it confuses the customers or worries them into backing away from a purchase.

Lanier's biggest asset is its sales force. While other business products companies pay salespeople straight salaries and small commissions, Lanier pays only commissions that range from 5 to 15 percent. Salespeople are further encouraged with large year-end bonuses for sales that exceed quota. In addition, Milner keeps Lanier's sales office spare. To make a phone call a salesperson must wait a turn at a row of phone cubicles along a wall -- this discourages long-winded chatting, according to Milner (Fortune, February 26, 1979).

In July 1978 Lanier was appointed to market Wordplex, a shared logic or clustered system, in the United States. Wordplex, a California-based company, was acquired by AES of Canada. Wordplex gives customers with large installations access to mass storage and data base at a low cost per typing station. The system has central disc storage for up to 70,000 pages. From Lanier's standpoint, the clustered system provides the ideal upgrade for its customers from the company's popular stand-alone machines.

The challenge facing Lanier in the next decade will be to successfully market larger systems. Despite Lanier's dazzling success there are some critics who doubt the company's ability to make the jump into larger, more complex systems. Richard Hastings of Merrill Lynch observed:

> I don't think Lanier will ever do anything with Wordplex. Their strength has been in the smaller systems. When you talk about larger systems, you're talking about a much bigger investment, so your salespeople have to talk to financial people and others higher up on the management ladder. It's a different game for Lanier, one where they're not experienced (Kulkowsky 1980).

Gene Milner points out that the company's strong marketing orientation will carry over more easily into the market for big-ticket clustered systems than the critics think. Milner's statement is more than just management bravado. According to IDC, in 1979 Lanier moved to second place in the clustered systems segment of the market, just one year after acquiring the distribution contract for Wordplex. On the strength of its past performance, no one is counting it out yet.

NBI

NBI is typical of the small technology-based companies that grew up in the 1970s to take advantage of the growing market for word processing. Unlike Vydec, Lexitron, and Micom, who had similar beginnings, NBI has not been acquired by a larger company. The company's innovative idea was to apply microprocessor technology to word processing machines. This meant that the equipment was programmable just like a minicomputer. As such NBI's machines could operate either as stand-alones or put together in clusters. This is the so-called modular approach to design, which also allows equipment to be used in a centralized or decentralized setting.

In 1975 a San Francisco venture capital firm provided the initial funds for NBI. The company's strategy was to sell rather than rent equipment to a small focused share of the market. There are four ingredients to NBI's sales approach: target market saturation, strong dealer representatives, OEM sales, and international distribution.

NBI initially opened direct sales offices in four key cities: Washington, Chicago, San Francisco, and Denver. Its plan was for each to become a major factor in a particular geographic market. Sales would then expand from this base (Seybold Report).

Second, NBI concentrated on finding strong distributors. The company realized it could not undertake widespread distribution of its equipment alone because of the heavy investment required in staffing and supporting branch operations. It turned instead to building a network of dealers who would provide a high level of service and support for its products. NBI carefully selects its dealers and will sell systems only to office equipment dealers who are already well established in their own markets and have sales revenues in excess of $1 million. The dealer is required to provide a certain level of staffing, to promote and support NBI products, and is assigned quotas based on size of market area serviced. In return, NBI grants exclusive territory.

NBI's most recent tactic involves branching out overseas. The company announced in May 1979 that it had reached an agreement with TRW, which will distribute NBI machines in 40 countries. The agreement runs for five years and requires TRW to purchase certain minimum numbers of machines throughout that period (Seybold Report).

NBI is also aggressively pursuing OEM sales. Recently the company announced that it will sell a custom version of its 3000 machine to Olivetti Corporation. The quality of NBI's products makes them a good choice as supplier to OEMs. In the future as direct sales to end users become more competitive, this could well be the market niche that NBI will pursue most aggressively.

- To maintain a strong position in the stand-alone display market, which is likely to become increasingly competitive with the entry of IBM and other large companies into this segment.
- To develop and market a clustered system to provide an upgrade path for its customers and to take advantage of the anticipated growth in this market.
- To address the management problem of integrating three small companies so that Exxon Office Systems can provide its customers with a broad range of office automation products and services.

Prime Computer, Inc.

Prime was founded in 1972 by seven Honeywell executives who left that company when Honeywell got out of the minicomputer business. Based on a high performance technology called MULTICS, which had been developed at MIT, Prime was able to come up with one of the early minicomputers that had the capabilities previously found only in large mainframe computers. Despite this technological breakthrough, the company was initially unable to competitively price its equipment or develop a successful sales strategy (company documents).

In 1975 Prime was able to lure Kenneth Fisher, a vice-president at Honeywell, to the chief executive job. Fisher's first move was to repackage the minis, adding peripheral devices to provide a complete system suitable for end users. Prime then expanded its sales force and concentrated its marketing effort on those scientific, engineering, and business customers who were sophisticated users of computer technology. Having in-house technical ability was an important customer trait, since Prime could not compete with companies like IBM on service.

From the beginning, Prime's equipment was designed to be interactive, that is, if a question is typed on the keyboard, the computer comes back with an answer or a request for more information. This encourages a kind of dialogue that is a popular feature with most users. In addition all of Prime's systems are interchangeable, thus making system upgrading or additions easy.

Prime's strategy of providing high-quality minicomputers to sophisticated users has brought the company tremendous growth in both sales and earnings. In 1975 sales were $11.5 million; by 1980 they were projected to reach $250 million.

Like most of the other minicomputer manufacturers such as DEC and Datapoint, Prime saw the importance of providing a word processing capability for its equipment. In April 1980 Prime announced its new Office Automation System. This product, based on the company's minicomputer technology, provides for the integration of word processing, electronic mail, calendar management, and data processing in one system.

Prime's sales strategy for its office automation system is similar to the successful tactics it has used in selling its data processing systems. Its strategy has been to target relatively sophisticated users of office automation equipment and provide them with high-quality integrated systems. The criteria it uses for targeting potential customers are:

- The company must be large, requiring a sophisticated system, and with the budget necessary to buy it.
- Since Prime sells such a large integrated system, it makes its sales pitch to top management and therefore targets companies that have a corporate-level person in charge of office automation decisions.

In 1979 IDC estimated that 20 percent of the Fortune 500 companies had such a person in place; by 1980 they estimated that the figure had reached 50 percent. In its sales approach Prime stresses the importance of making managers as well as secretaries more productive and emphasizes that its multifunction approach is likely to be far more cost effective and result in greater application.

Prime is aiming at the high end or multifunction segment of the market. This strategy is consistent with the company's expertise in minicomputers and integrated systems. It has had some early success in selling its systems, having placed them at Lincoln National Life Insurance Company and an Air Force installation at Hanscom Field in Bedford, Massachusetts.

Like Wang, Prime is a young company that has to deal with the challenge of growth. The risk of Prime's marketing strategy is that there are not enough sophisticated users who will buy a complete system and that movement toward an integrated system is likely to come about by adding and combining equipment as a company gains expertise.

However, indications are that there will be a growing demand for multifunction integrated systems. The experience Prime is gaining now should help it as more companies become ready to invest in large integrated systems. Prime's impressive performance in the minicomputer market makes it a company to watch in the next decade in this growing segment of the word processing market.

Summary

In this section we have examined the competitive strategies of a sample of firms competing in the word processing industry. We have seen the variety of product and business backgrounds of these firms. Some, like Lanier, had a base of office products customers but had virtually no experience in selling either type-writers or computer-based systems. Others, such as Wang and Prime, had strong technical expertise and a good position in the minicomputer market but no experience selling to the traditional office products market. Yet all of these companies saw the tremendous opportunities for growth and profit in the word pro-cessing market and each brought its own particular expertise, style, and strategy to the market. Some, like Vydec and Lanier, concentrated on gaining market share in those segments where demand was strongest. Others, like Prime, were putting together more sophisticated systems to take advantage of their own expertise and the expected future trends in the market.

Up to this point the overall growth in demand has provided enough business for everyone. Yet the signs indicate that some changes are taking place: More firms are competing for the word processing dollar in all segments of the market. Price cutting, led by IBM and Wang, is taking place in the stand-alone display segment. Customers are increasingly concerned not only with the quality and service provided by the vendor, but also the degree to which the equipment is upgradeable and whether the manufacturers can provide support for integrating a variety of office automation technologies.

We now turn to a closer examination of what industry observers suggest will be the future trends in word processing.

FUTURE TRENDS: FROM WORD PROCESSING TO THE OFFICE OF THE FUTURE?

The development and subsequent diffusion of word processing technology has exposed the traditional office to the power of computerized systems and the potential for radical change. Just as the widespread use of the typewriter brought about other advances in office machinery and organizational design, so the widespread use of word processing has brought about other innovations in office products and office work and probably will continue to do so. The word processor is to the automated office of the future what the mainframe computer was to data processing: a major product innovation that was the foundation for other technological developments (IDC).

Word processing technology itself has evolved from its position in the early 1970s as a typewriter replacement to a much broader information processing tool. The concept of combining word and data processing began to change the nature of word processing for vendors and users alike. Instead of remaining an instrument for editing text, by combining word processing with other functions, a much more powerful technology is evolving.

The automated office represents the interconnection of all the means by which people communicate with each other and other offices. Businesses are discovering the potential of integrated information systems that go beyond simple text editing, communicating with the computer, and sending messages electronically.

Both companies that have traditionally approached the office from the data processing angle and those coming from word processing have begun to integrate systems. The dollar volume for the major types of office automation equipment during 1979 show that word processors led all types of equipment with $1.03 billion in shipments (see Figure 4.10). The word processing market has been the earliest segment of the office automation market to achieve substantial dollar volume. In 1979 word processing made up 89 percent of the total office automation equipment market, which includes fascimile, intelligent copiers, and teleconferencing equipment.

Changes are occurring both at the low and the high ends of the word processing market. The advent of electronic typewriters with memory will have the effect of redistributing some market share away from certain segments of the word processing market such as the stand-alone display and nondisplay segment. Hybrid systems that combine word and data processing into one system will also have this result. Already price competition in this segment of the market has caused companies to cut back on service and training support (Business Week, November 1980).

International Data Corporation predicts that demand for word processing will continue to grow strongly, but that demand for other types of office automation equipment will be even stronger, thus word processing should make up 75 percent of total office automation demand by 1984. The greatest growth in the word processing market is predicted to be in the clustered and hybrid systems segment.

Based on Abernathy and Utterback's (1978) model of technology evolution, it would appear that at least in some segments of the market a "dominant product design" has appeared. Certain product characteristics — such as the video screen, the microprocessor modular design pioneered by NBI, and the use of English-like commands — have become standard product features.

In looking at the development of word processing technology, we can see that entry barriers were low and that a variety of firms took advantage of this opportunity to compete in a

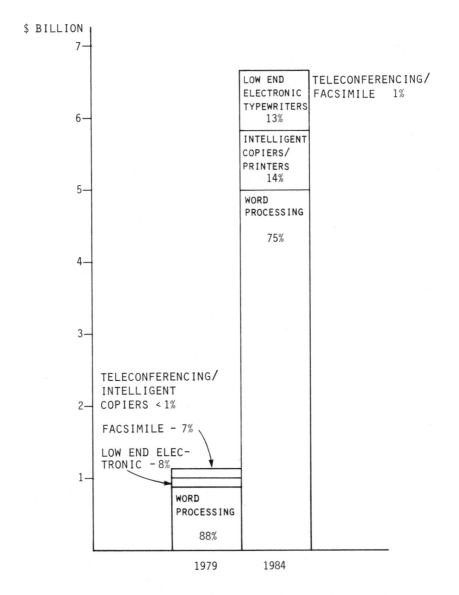

FIGURE 4.10
Future Trends

By 1984, equipment shipments will climb to $6.7 billion. This does not include software, services, or supplies (or consulting).

Source: IDC.

growing and lucrative market. In terms of the technology life cycle, the product seems to be at a "transition stage" where performance characteristics are becoming more defined, price competition is increasing, and sales volumes are expanding rapidly. In terms of the implementation issue under study, it does not appear that failure to fully utilize the equipment has been caused by product offerings that have not found market acceptance. At least at the level of initial adoption, word processing technology seems to be diffusing rapidly. As the technology has evolved in the past decade, so too has its use and application within business organizations. The following chapters will examine how a sample of user organizations purchased and subsequently utilized the technology. By analyzing their experiences we will address the research questions posed earlier and make some assessments about the evolution of word processing from both the users' and the vendors' perspective.

5
THE CASE STUDIES: EXAMINING THE IMPLEMENTATION OF WORD PROCESSING TECHNOLOGY IN THREE ORGANIZATIONS

This chapter examines the implementation of word processing technology in three organizations: Williamsburg Clothiers (disguised name), Corning Glass Works, and Lincoln National Life Insurance Company. Each company represents a different hypothetical stage of evolution toward full implementation. The first section describes each company's initial purchase and use of word processing technology, subsequent changes, and issues for future consideration.

The second section focuses on the changes that occurred in the four variables outlined in the conceptual framework: the purchase decision criteria, technology, portfolio of technology use, and organizational structure.

The final section examines the implementation strategies of these three firms, going beyond the structured interview questions to develop a better understanding of the culture of the firms and the demands of their competitive environments. Miles and Kimberly (1980) suggest that "organizations cannot be fully understood apart from their histories." This section explores the relationship between each firm's historical experience and its choice of implementation strategies.

THE CASES

Williamsburg Clothiers

Background of the Company

Williamsburg Clothiers was founded by Mary Flavin in 1945, shortly after her husband was killed in action during World War

II. Mrs. Flavin and her daughters began operating a small specialty shop in the two front parlors of their gracious colonial home in historic Williamsburg, Virginia. When Mrs. Flavin died suddenly in 1950, her oldest daughter Elizabeth and son-in-law John Alden took over the business. In 1955 the company moved to a large well-appointed store in downtown Williamsburg and opened another store in Charlottesville, Virginia.

In conjunction with their successful store operations, the Aldens embarked on the development of a mail-order business, distributing flyers and placing ads in several national magazines. During the ensuing years, Williamsburg Clothiers enjoyed a modest rate of growth, a high rate of profitability, and a strong reputation for quality and service. This combination of assets made the company an attractive candidate for acquisition, and in 1973 John and Elizabeth Alden sold the business to a large conglomerate.

Williamsburg now operates as a wholly owned subsidiary of that firm while enjoying relative autonomy in its day-to-day operations. Since its acquisition, the company has pursued a more aggressive growth strategy. By 1980 the mail-order business had expanded from 3,000 black and white flyers to over 15 million flyers annually. In addition, the company has 15 stores throughout Virginia, Maryland, and the fast-growing Piedmont region of the Carolinas. Sales more than tripled between 1976 and 1980 (see Table 5.1).

The Company's Business

Williamsburg Clothiers is a retailer of high-quality classic clothing for women and men. The company buys its merchandise from about 500 leading vendors and distributes it through its 15 retail stores and through the six major catalogs mailed annually.

Although the business has grown dramatically since the early days when Mrs. Flavin and her daughters personally knew most of their customers, Williamsburg Clothiers still prides itself on an exceptional degree of personal service. Maintaining a close relationship with customers and responding to unusual or unique requests is an integral part of Williamsburg's strategy. The following story is an example of the company's commitment to meeting customer needs: A contessa in Spain sent a linen handkerchief and asked if Williamsburg's monogramming department could copy the unique embroidered crest on six oxford cloth shirts to wear horseback riding. The company's skilled artists did them for her, making sure to heed her directions, "Remember, nine points on the crown for a contessa!"

On another occasion the head of the Peace Corps in Micronesia wrote and asked if the company could suggest a suitable wardrobe for her work and traveling. She traveled in

TABLE 5.1

Williamsburg Clothiers, Financial and Sales Data, 1976–84

	Actual					Plan		
	1976	1977	1978	1979	1980	1981	1982	1984
	(in thousands of dollars)							
Current assets	1,702	1,557	1,772	3,981	6,336			
Current liabilities	941	612	2,208	3,026	6,233			
Long-term debt	302	292	281	271	260			
Equity	2,231	2,622	3,861	5,674	7,565			
Fixed assets (net)	2,068	2,059	2,542	4,329	11,228			
	(in millions of dollars)							
Retail sales	3.0	3.8	4.7	8.0	12.5	19.0	25.7	57.0
Catalog sales	6.6	7.0	13.7	22.3	28.0	34.2	40.4	54.0
Total sales	9.6	10.8	18.4	30.3	40.5	53.2	66.1	111.0
Return on sales (percent)	7.6	5.5	10.4	9.2	6.4	7.4	7.9	7.9
Retail (percent)	17.6	17.0	19.5	20.4	18.6	16.5	15.8	14.3
Catalog (percent)	10.4	7.9	13.4	11.6	8.8	10.0	10.5	10.5
General and administrative (percent)	5.0	5.7	4.6	4.8	5.4	4.9	4.7	4.6
Number of retail stores	5	5	6	8	11	17	25	49

jungles, but women wearing slacks were frowned upon; hence she needed wrap skirts and cool cotton shirts in specific materials and colors. Williamsburg people clipped pictures of suitable items and put together a minicatalog broken down into work, travel, evening wear, and casual clothes. She ordered $1,060 worth of clothing as a result and was very appreciative of their assistance.

Organization of Operations

With the exception of the 15 retail store managers and their sales staffs, all of Williamsburg's personnel are located at company headquarters. Operations can be broken down into three general areas: management and support personnel, catalog order processing, and receiving and distribution of merchandise.

The Williamsburg, Virginia, headquarters houses about 80 management personnel charged with the various line and staff responsibilities outlined in Figure 5.1.

Initial Experience with Word Processing

In March 1978 the manager of Customer Services at Williamsburg recommended that the company purchase a Wang System 20 word processor. It was used initially as a stand-alone system, with one work station and one Diablo printer.

Initially the primary use of the system was for "merge letters" providing correspondence for Customer Service and Accounts Receivable and replies from Personnel to applicants for employment. In the past some of this work had been subcontracted out to local printers or typing services depending on demand.

Williamsburg management had traditionally emphasized the importance of keeping correspondence and communications as simple as possible. The company was beginning to grow rapidly at the same time that the new technology was introduced, and there was an increased demand for general clerical and administrative support.

The use of word processing technology was quickly expanded beyond the customer service function to cover a much broader range of correspondence and report writing. Within two years of its initial purchase, Williamsburg upgraded its equipment to a Wang System 30, a clustered system that was installed with five work stations and two printers.

In a short period Office Services was providing a wide range of typing support, to headquarters staff as well as Customer Services. The organization was "discovering" word processing, and the idea of a central Office Services group seemed to be

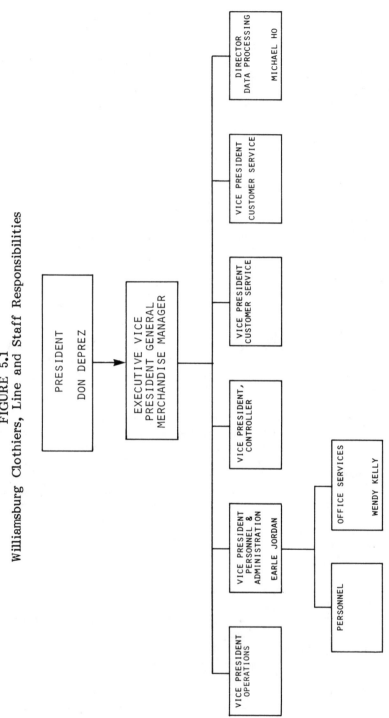

FIGURE 5.1
Williamsburg Clothiers, Line and Staff Responsibilities

PRESIDENT
DON DEPREZ

EXECUTIVE VICE
PRESIDENT GENERAL
MERCHANDISE MANAGER

VICE PRESIDENT
OPERATIONS

VICE PRESIDENT
PERSONNEL &
ADMINISTRATION
EARLE JORDAN

VICE PRESIDENT,
CONTROLLER

VICE PRESIDENT
CUSTOMER SERVICE

VICE PRESIDENT
CUSTOMER SERVICE

DIRECTOR
DATA PROCESSING
MICHAEL HO

PERSONNEL

OFFICE SERVICES
WENDY KELLY

generally accepted. Wendy Kelly, the department manager, felt that the reasons for this success were good equipment and excellent service, with technically capable operators who had good proof-reading skills.

By early 1980 a full night shift had been added to handle Customer Service correspondence -- the original reason for purchasing the equipment. Since the company was already beginning to think about adding work stations or upgrading the technology, it wanted to reevaluate the idea of a centralized Office Services group before moving into a new headquarters building in 1980 and committing itself to that layout.

From the beginning, Wendy Kelly and her Office Services staff perceived their job as one of encouraging clients to use word processing for a variety of needs. She had no doubt that Williamsburg would need still more word processing capacity, both in the short run and in the longer term. Each new store that was added generated an increase both in retail sales and in catalog orders, while the headquarters staff continued to grow.

With five work stations, Office Services already had to queue projects and ask clients to specify the longest acceptable turn-around times on their specific projects. Since it was almost impossible to determine how much the system was actually being used for "excessive" or unnecessary work, Wendy had discussed with her boss, Earle Jordan, some kind of chargeout system that would penalize users for too many "urgent" requests.

As Office Services continued to expand both in number of operators and equipment, its budget increased at a faster rate than sales revenue. The issue, as Williamsburg saw it, was one of control. Management felt that use of word processing should be encouraged, but only to the point of providing necessary typing services in a cost-efficient manner.

Future Considerations

A possible solution to the control issue was to decentralize some of the word processing functions of Office Services into the individual departments, giving the users there responsibility for priority setting and cost control. A drawback to central-ization might be that it would encourage a proliferation of equipment throughout the organization and ultimately become more costly than a well-managed central facility. Decentral-ization also might compromise the consistent quality of writing and proof-reading that Office Services provided.

As an alternative possibility, operators within the central group might be assigned to specific departments, allowing them to become familiar with the particular terms, procedures, and business of a departmental group. One manager mentioned to the author that the range of general work that operators in a centralized system performed prevented them from developing the specific competence needed within a given department, and the kind of "shorthand" communication in a traditional manager/secretary relationship did not occur.

Some managers felt that explaining work to operators took more of their time, resulting in higher costs or more inefficiency, than in the traditional office. They made a similar observation about changes in the practice of managers keeping their own files.

The alternative of encouraging operators to develop closer relationships with the individual departments could also build career paths there for promoting operators from Office Services. Williamsburg was still a small company and there were not many positions to move into in Office Services or Personnel and Administration.

Williamsburg's data processing department had not been involved in any of the technology decisions made by the Office Services group. As new capabilities, such as electronic mail or localized computing, became available on some of Wang's more sophisticated models, Wendy wondered whether Office Services should try to establish a closer link to the company's data processing group.

For the moment, however, Williamsburg's principal concern was to continue to provide quality service in word processing without losing cost efficiency.

Corning Glass Works

Background of the Company

Since its founding in the mid-nineteenth century, Corning Glass Works, in Corning, New York, has built a strong reputation as a manufacturer and marketer of specialty glass. Corning's stated corporate objective is "to pursue excellence in glass worldwide, making the family of materials, its related products, and its corollary technologies the most unusual and useful in our civilization." This strategy, built around a material and its applications, had led Corning to focus on technology-based research as the core of the company's operation. The company's reputation, growth, and profitability are thus based on technological innovation and efficient manufacturing capabilities.

Corning Glass Works produces a wide variety of products that can be grouped into four industry segments:

- Consumer Products: Tableware and houseware made from heat-resistant glass and glass ceramic compositions.

- Consumer Durable Components: Components used in the manu-
facture of consumer goods such as television bulbs, ceramic
substrates, and lighting products.
- Capital Goods Components: Components for products linked to
capital investment, such as refractories, chemical process
systems, electronic products, and optical waveguides.
- Health and Science: Products related to the health and lab-
oratory fields, such as clinical instruments, diagnostic testing
systems, and optical and ophthalmic products.

Corning manufactures products in ten countries, has sales
offices in many more, and has equity holdings in 12 principal
associated companies worldwide. Total 1979 corporate sales were
about $1.4 billion with net income of about $125 million. International operations accounted for about 28 percent of sales and
about 11 percent of net income.

Organization

Corning is organized along product lines with the International Division managing all international operations. The
Finance, Legal, Personnel, Research and Development, Distribution
and Information Services divisions are all centralized at Corning
corporate headquarters (see Figure 5.2). Most other division
vice-presidents also have their offices and staffs located in
Corning. The major manufacturing sites are also in the vicinity.
In 1978 the company set up the Information Systems Division
(ISD), a corporate-level staff function responsible for assisting
the various divisions in managing information and overseeing
certain administrative departments. Reporting to the director of
the ISD were the heads of Data Processing, Telecommunications,
and Administrative Services. The head of Administrative Services
was responsible for office services, the physical mail system, food
services, and certain other related functions (see Figure 5.3).

Initial Experience with Word Processing

Corning's initial experience with word processing technology
began in the individual product divisions, which used centralized
typing pools with two or three people to handle lengthy or
repetitive documents. By 1972, when IBM's MagCard machines
had become widely available, some of these divisions decided to
lease the equipment for their typing pools on a trial basis. The
initial decision to invest in word processing technology was made
by individual managers and administrative support people within
the line divisions.

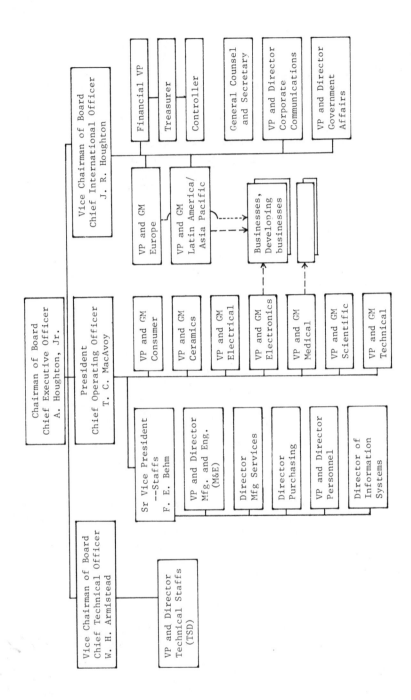

FIGURE 5.2
Corning Glass Works, Corporate Structure

FIGURE 5.3
Corning Glass Works, Information Systems Division

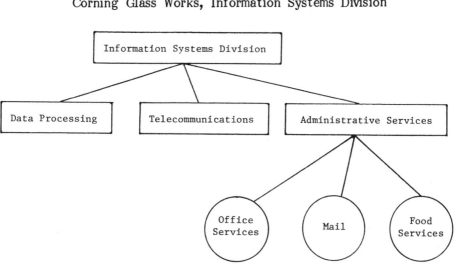

In the mid-1970s, as more word processing technologies became available, the various product divisions at Corning turned to the corporate-level Administrative Services group for assistance in planning and implementing a strategy to improve overall office productivity. As a result, the Finance, Legal, Medical, and Personnel Divisions were the first to install communications centers on separate floors of one building in 1976 and 1977. Secretarial and clerical work was restructured to emphasize the potential of word processing technology for improving efficiency and eliminating some jobs. The basic concept of this strategy was to make two separate jobs out of the principal secretarial functions of typing and administrative support.

Although people working in the communications centers reported directly to Administrative Services, they identified more closely with the operating divisions on the floors where they were assigned and thought of their jobs as providing service to clients there.

Corning's initial experience with these communications centers revealed that not as many secretaries were laid off as had been anticipated. They began doing different kinds of administrative work; and communications centers even began to take on certain administrative functions that could be easily centralized, such as mail distribution, coffee making, copying, conference room scheduling, and so on.

This was an opportunity for people to rethink how they did their jobs. When Administrative Services undertook a study on the possibility of installing a communications center in the International Division, the focus shifted to improving the effectiveness of both managers and secretaries in a particular department, and to realizing cost savings by delegation of work rather than eliminating some positions. In confidential interviews, managers and employees were asked which tasks they felt they could delegate to subordinates and which could be delegated to them from superiors.

Future Considerations

The most critical aspect for the future, according to Jack Lesser, manager of Administrative Services, was that managers continue to accept the concept that the technology provides the opportunity for a better and more cost-effective restructuring of work. He felt there was still great potential in the delegation process and predicted that the communications center concept could probably be further decentralized as administrative aides and executives began to use terminals themselves. He saw the Administrative Services role as one of providing guidance and expertise, leaving it to the users themselves to define their own needs, initiate purchase and use of equipment, and manage the necessary working relationships.

Lincoln National Life Insurance Company

Background of the Company

Lincoln National Life is part of the Lincoln National Corporation, which provides life/health insurance and annuities, property casualty insurance, and related services. The Lincoln National Corporation includes Lincoln National Life, Security- Connecticut Life Insurance Company, Dominion Life Assurance Company of Canada, American State Insurance Company, and Chicago Title and Trust. Of these companies, Lincoln National Life is the largest, contributing over 65 percent of total revenue.

Lincoln Life serves two major markets: direct agency sales to individuals and businesses and reinsurance to other life insurance companies. Lincoln Life operates 87 life insurance agencies and manages over 3,000 career agents. The company is the fifth largest U.S. stock life insurer and its reinsurance operation is the largest in the country. Reinsurance sales increased by 45 percent between 1978 and 1979, partly because of Lincoln's aggressive sales strategy and partly because the very large policy (several million dollars of face amount) segment of the market that Lincoln has served most effectively has grown the fastest. In 1979 total revenue for the Lincoln National Corporation from both insurance and investment sources exceeded

$2.4 billion. Company headquarters are located in Fort Wayne, Indiana, and house about 3,500 Lincoln Life employees.

Initial Experience with Word Processing Technology, 1968-78

The concept of centralized word processing was not new to the insurance industry or to Lincoln Life. Before text-editing technology became widely available, Lincoln had used a central typing pool to process the large amount of correspondence to agents and policyholders, which was an essential part of the insurance business. While a typical manager outside of the insurance industry might dictate three to four letters per day, a manager in the Client Services Department of an insurance company might dictate as many as 30 to 40 letters per day. This created the need to process large volumes of correspondence, which led to the establishment of a word processing center.

Lincoln's original IBM MT/ST machines did not allow for simultaneous input and output and could not be cost justified. The manager of Word Processing, however, was farsighted enough to realize that the technology had potential for improving output and efficiency.

Lincoln upgraded its word processing technology, first to MagCard I's in 1976 to allow for simultaneous input and output, and in the following year to the IBM OS/6, which could hold up to 130 text pages in storage. With this new equipment the Word Processing Center was able to handle a somewhat broader range of applications, but it continued to function mainly as a centralized typing pool for correspondence with policyholders and agents. Operators had little contact with the client group and their basic tasks remained unchanged for ten years.

1978 Corporate Priority to Productivity Improvement

Like many other insurance companies in 1978, Lincoln found its profit margins were being squeezed by the twin problems of rising inflation rates and spiraling costs. To attack these two problems, Lincoln's top management established as a major corporate objective the achievement of a substantial improvement in productivity. The goal was to maintain staff levels while increasing the volume of business.

The company embarked on a "Quality Commitment" program that was aimed at making fundamental changes in the way the company operated its business. Instead of fragmenting many jobs into specialized tasks, Quality Commitment was aimed at designing broader and more interesting jobs that would capitalize on the motivational needs and expertise of employees while simplifying organizational structures and processes.

The program, initiated and developed by the president and senior management, brought about massive change at Lincoln. Several departments were completely reorganized. These changes demonstrated that substantial savings were possible even as workloads increased. Morale was improved in the process and turnover reduced. In 1979, after increasing 10-15 percent for many years, staff levels did not increase at all, while total revenue increased by 11 percent and net income gained by 8 percent.

While the Senior Staff Committee was developing its plan for Quality Commitment, the data processing department was developing a five-year strategic plan aimed at productivity improvement that called for:

- elimination of 90 percent of the paper generated internally at Lincoln -- the goal was for more information, not paper;
- establishment of distributed data processing, utilizing a terminal as a work station-level computer.

The R&D group within Data Processing began to explore various technology alternatives that would bring the company closer to meeting these long-term strategic goals. In early 1979 they brought a proposal to Dave Allen, director of Data Processing, requesting $500,000 to develop a prototype of an automated office using Prime hardware and software developed by ACS, a software development house in New York. Allen authorized the project.

It was then determined by the Senior Staff Committee that R&D's development of the automated office and Data Processing's plan for distributed data processing should be considered one project. Top management then established that the various kinds of information required to run an insurance company should be brought under one umbrella. At this point, Office Services, Telecommunications, and Data Processing merged under the senior vice-president of Data Processing. Allen was promoted to this job.

The development of the automated office was given the clear goal of incorporating the objectives of the data processing plan. Effort was concentrated on developing a multifunction terminal that could simultaneously provide computational power, text editing, electronic mail, and file management.

In early 1980, 30 to 40 terminals were installed in Data Processing to see if the system would actually work and to iron out any existing problems. After a favorable response here, the system got its first bona fide pilot test in the Law Department, where 70 terminals and printers were installed in the spring of 1980.

The Law Department proved to be a good pilot location since it was in the process of installing Lexis, a large computerized data base of legal research, and was enthusiastic and willing to use the new technology. Once the system became available for use, the president and almost all the top-level managers began using the terminals.

At this point an Automated Office Systems group was moved out of R&D and established to market the system to potential users and to provide training, planning, and technical support. An example of the Automated Office Systems group's responsibilities include establishment of a Steering Committee charged with system implementation. In the case of the Law Department, Automated Office Systems established a committee consisting of three attorneys, a technical support person, a person from Automated Office Systems, a person from R&D, a person from Telecommunications, and one from Human Resources to plan, design, and implement the system. The Automated Office Services manager that the casewriter talked to described the planning process as a wheel. "You go back forever to continually update the system, the training, and the support required."

Lincoln's plan was to use a "soft sell" approach, picking the most receptive areas of the company, and generating demand for systems through the enthusiasm of the pilot users. The system began to penetrate the organization from the top down. For example, once the senior vice-president of Finance began using the system and sending messages through electronic mail, managers in the Tax and Control areas found it necessary to get their own terminals, just to be able to talk to their boss.

Lincoln's goal was to install 1,500 terminals by the end of 1983. By the end of 1980 they already had 300 in place.

Centralized Word Processing and the Automated Office

The massive changes occurring at Lincoln as a result of the Quality Commitment program and the Automated Office System also affected the centralized Word Processing group. Operators formed work groups responsible for handling all the work for a particular department or set of users, so that they would know the people behind the work they typed and become more familiar with a particular branch of the insurance industry. In some cases, a group of operators was physically moved to the client's location to provide for closer contact and better service.

The work groups themselves, rather than a supervisor, were responsible for scheduling their own work, vacation days, and other personal time. The work groups were also involved in evaluating titles, pay rates, and operating procedures for the department. In keeping with the job-enrichment principles of Quality Commitment, people were trained to operate all of the equipment used in the department, MagCard machines, laser printers, as well as the new Automated Office Services terminals that were being installed on a trial basis.

By 1980 the Word Processing Center had roughly 43 employees and processed about 20,000 pages per month. Policy-holder and agent correspondence was still the principal job of the center, although closer contact with client groups and the acquisition of some new technologies had broadened the range of service that the center provided. Some Automated Office Services terminals had been installed in the Word Processing Center on a trial basis, mainly as a means of communication between operators and clients. For example, a user might dictate a letter from his or her phone to the Central Dictating bank that Word Processing maintained. An operator would transcribe the work on a terminal and then send the completed copy via electronic mail back to the user, who could then correct it, send it on electronically, or have it printed. In this way the Word Processing group became linked through the Automated Office Systems network with the entire company.

Future Considerations

Lincoln's plans for the future called for using the Automated Office Services to link the company's field agents and subsidiary companies like Chicago Title and Trust, with corporate head-quarters. Management was concerned that the Automated Office Services not be seen exclusively as a "staff" tool just because the various staff functions at headquarters had been the first group to use it. They were now interested in getting the operating groups and field agencies on line.

*   *   *

In the following section we will examine the experiences of these three companies in terms of the four variables of the conceptual framework: the purchase decision criteria, technology, portfolio of technology use, and organizational structure. We will use the descriptive data as a basis for determining if there appear to be general patterns of experience for the purchase and use of word processing technology that are analogous to the evolutionary stages models outlined in the conceptual framework.

EXAMINING THE CASE DATA IN TERMS OF THE FOUR VARIABLES OF THE CONCEPTUAL FRAMEWORK

The Purchase Decision Criteria

Williamsburg Clothiers was a relative latecomer to the use of word processing technology, making its first purchase of a Wang System 20 in 1978. The company's decision to buy the equipment was prompted by the need to keep up with the rising volume of customer correspondence brought about by the expansion of branch stores and catalog sales. In addition to the need for quick response to an increased volume of work, Williamsburg was also concerned that customers would receive a professional-looking high-quality letter.

The need to stem rising costs and at the same time continue to provide quality output were the principal reasons that Williamsburg made the initial investment in word processing technology. Prior to this the company had relied on the services of contracted typists or printing companies to meet what was then sporadic rather than steady demand.

Although Williamsburg expanded its use of word processing equipment in a fairly short period of time, the company's purchase decision criteria did not change significantly. Williamsburg was still primarily concerned with controlling costs while meeting both customer and in-house demands for text output. While Williamsburg management was certainly aware of such issues as increasing management productivity or providing more decentralized service, they viewed the acquisition and use of word processing as a tool to improve secretarial productivity.

Corning's initial experience with word processing was quite similar. When individual product divisions began leasing IBM MT/ST and MagCard machines for use in division typing pools, the major reasons for the investment were the desire to meet the demands for more text output and at the same time make better use of secretarial time, thereby controlling growing clerical costs.

At Corning this concept changed. Management now views word processing as a tool for greater managerial productivity. Managers have learned to use the technology as a catalyst for pushing down each task to the lowest possible level in the corporation. Most of the heavy typing was removed from the private secretary/administrative assistant to a central communications center. Relieved of the typing responsibility, secretaries could begin to do some of the work previously done by managers. Managers, in turn, were free to spend more of their time on jobs that specifically required their skills. Corning management estimated that effective delegation of work would bring about the greatest increases in overall productivity.

Lincoln's initial investment in word processing technology was in 1968. The first machines, IBM MT/STs, were installed in the company's central typing pool, which handled most of the routine policyholder and agent correspondence. Although the machines could not at first be cost justified, managers recognized the potential of the technology to save operator time and eventually print out correspondence more quickly.

After ten years, word processing at Lincoln was incorporated into an Automated Office System designed to increase productivity at all levels in the corporation. Distributed word processing and distributed data processing were now seen as tools for increasing both secretarial and managerial productivity. The central Word Processing group is now incorporated within the Automated Office System network.

In two out of the three case sites, emphasis shifted away from looking at the technology as a tool for greater secretarial productivity and text output. Corning and Lincoln became more concerned with using the technology for increased effectiveness and managerial productivity. This change in emphasis reflected a different concept of the technology itself. Instead of viewing word processing as a typewriter replacement, it came to be viewed, at least in two companies, as a tool for increased communications and managerial productivity, either by itself or in conjunction with other office automation technologies.

In this initial diffusion of word processing technology, the innovation was perceived as having the five attributes identified by Rogers and Shoemaker as necessary for success (see Chapter 2):

A word processor did have relative advantage over typewriters in terms of faster output and saving operator time. Even the early machines, such as Lincoln's original IBM MT/ST, had the potential of eventually justifying their high initial cost through increased productivity.

The equipment was compatible with existing procedures and operations since it was usually introduced into existing typing pools to replace typewriters. It did not initially disrupt traditional manager/secretary relationships.

The complexity of the innovation required special training and experience in its early stages. Word processors became easier to use as they were modified and improved.

They were usually introduced in trial settings, in typing pools or correspondence centers.

The innovation was easy to observe in practice. Managers soon saw that revisions could be made quickly and that form letters, stored in machine memory, could speed the process of answering customer correspondence or writing reports.

Technology

Williamsburg management chose the Wang System 20, a stand-alone display unit, for its first word processing purchase. It had these advantages for the company:

- The quality of its output, closely resembling the IBM Selectric, was best suited to customer correspondence.
- Wang's shared logic capability made it easily upgradeable.
- Use of floppy discs made retrieval easy from up to 80 pages of storage.
- Software was more advanced or versatile.

The clustered system that the company installed a short time later was a central processing unit that could accommodate up to 14 peripheral devices such as work stations and printers and had a storage capacity of up to 4,000 pages. The system was easy to upgrade and Wang remained Williamsburg's only vendor.

Corning considered Wang as a potential supplier but chose IBM because of its unequaled ability to provide service to a relatively isolated location. IBM was also the company's principal data processing vendor.

Corning's first purchase was IBM MagCard equipment, which it began to upgrade to a clustered system, the IBM OS/6. DEC and Four Phase supplied some additional equipment, but IBM remained the company's principal vendor. Like Williamsburg, Corning upgraded to a clustered word processor, but by 1980 had not yet begun to link data processing and word processing.

Lincoln also chose IBM as its first vendor of word processing equipment, again because IBM was the only supplier that serviced Fort Wayne, Indiana, in 1968. Lincoln first purchased MT/ST machines and upgraded to MagCard equipment in 1976. With the purchase of an IBM OS/6, a CRT-based machine using floppy discs, it could handle the in-house telephone directory and other record-keeping activities.

Lincoln's automated office system represented a dramatic change in equipment. The company incorporated word processing into a multifunction terminal that was part of a distributed word and data processing network. To do this, Lincoln brought in a new vendor -- Prime. While IBM still supplied "dumb" terminals and OS/6 equipment, the software and central processing unit for the automated office system were purchased from Prime. Prime's particular expertise was in integrated multifunction systems and it appeared to be the only vendor who at that time could adequately meet Lincoln's specifications for an automated office system.

Portfolio of Use

In each of the three companies in the case study, use of the equipment expanded from its original purpose to include a broader range of applications. Williamsburg expanded its use of word processing equipment to include a greater variety of correspondence and general typing. The word processors were used for typing labels for catalog mailings, financial reports, procedure manuals, and ordinary business correspondence.

Corning expanded its use of the technology as well. Once the communications centers were set up, they handled virtually all of their clients' typing needs except the one- and two-page documents still typed by administrative assistants. In addition, word processing was seen as a catalyst for organizational change.

Lincoln incorporated word processing technology into an overall automated office system. Multifunction terminals handled both word and data processing and the number of systems users expanded dramatically.

Organizational Structure

At Williamsburg the first word processing equipment served the specific needs of the Customer Services Department, with operators reporting to its manager. Williamsburg's volume of correspondence was growing and the equipment was purchased largely to keep up with demand. Since it was used to replace the use of printing services or contracted typists, there was no plan to eliminate clerical jobs. An operator did have to be trained to use the word processor, but the basic content of the job, typing letters, and the pay rate did not change.

At Corning the first word processing equipment was brought into the typing pools of various product divisions. Here again, equipment was used to meet an increased volume of work within a particular division. Initially, no clerical positions were eliminated and operators reported to local division or product managers.

At Lincoln the original equipment was introduced within the company's central typing pool, which handled almost all policyholder and agent correspondence and operators' jobs remained pretty much the same. No clerical positions were eliminated. Word processing operators did report to an administrative manager -- that is, a person in charge of the typing pool itself, rather than a division or product manager.

At Williamsburg and Corning, word processing groups were located within the specific departments that they served and in close physical proximity to their clients. Operators reported to the local product or division managers. At Lincoln the equipment was originally placed in a central typing pool location. This meant that managers and secretaries from different departments came to a central location to get work done.

In terms of organizational structure we could say that word processing at Williamsburg and Corning was "decentralized" and reported to a "local" manager who had various other responsibilities. At Lincoln, word processing was "centrally" located and reported to an administrative manager, whose principal responsibility was to oversee word processing.

The introduction and expanded use of word processing technology had an impact on clerical jobs in all three organizations. The principal impact was the change in skills required of operators. At Williamsburg word processing equipment eliminated some of the more tedious aspects of traditional typing, such as manually centering headings, spacing footnotes, and "whiting out" mistakes, but the new technology required a different and somewhat more technical set of skills. Operators had to develop expertise in electronic file entry and retrieval so that the storage capability of floppy discs or central processing units could be fully utilized. At Corning communications center operators also developed these skills, and the traditional structured job changed as well. Secretaries became responsible for more decision-making and administrative tasks than was previously the case.

At Lincoln, where word processing was incorporated within a sophisticated office automation system, operators as well as managers began to develop programming skills as administrative skills and jobs changed.

Table 5.2 summarizes the experiences of these three companies in terms of the changes observed in the four variables of the conceptual framework. We can see that all three companies aligned along certain parameters. For example, each company upgraded its technology and expanded the applications of the equipment within the organization.

On the variable of purchase decision criteria, Corning and Lincoln did shift their view of the technology away from typing productivity to a broader notion of improving overall productivity and using the technology to support a wide range of administrative activity. Williamsburg retained its view of the technology as a typewriter replacement and continued to think about the purchasing decision in terms of typing productivity.

On another critical variable -- impact on management jobs -- both Corning and Lincoln had evolved along this dimension to using the technology as part of an overall plan to restructure work and improve productivity. At Williamsburg the technology was not viewed as a tool to support a wide range of management and professional activity and therefore word processing had no impact on the content or nature of management jobs.

TABLE 5.2
Summary of Case Experiences

	Williamsburg	Corning	Lincoln
Initial purchase decision criteria	Improve typing productivity	Improve typing productivity	Improve typing productivity
Changes	No	Yes: Improve overall productivity	Yes: Improve overall productivity
Initial technology	Stand-alone display unit	IBM MagCard machine	IBM MT/ST
Changes	Yes: Clustered system	Yes: Stand-alone display/clustered system	Yes: Multifunction automated office system
Initial technology use	Customer correspondence — form letters	Form letters/repetitive typing	Policyholder/agent correspondence
Changes	Yes: Broad range of typing applications	Yes: Broad range of typing	Yes: Word/data processing functions merged
Organizational structure/initial location of word processing	Decentralized/local manager	Decentralized/local	Centralized/corporate
Changes	Yes: Centralized/ corporate	Yes: Decentralized/ corporate	Yes: Decentralized/ corporate
Impact on line management jobs	No	Yes	Yes

Within the terms of our definition of "successful" implementation, Williamsburg remained a fairly immature user because of its exclusive emphasis on "mechanizing" the typing function. This was true even though Williamsburg had upgraded its technology and had a fairly sophisticated Wang clustered system.

Lincoln Life was the most mature user of the technology in that it was able to integrate word processing with other technologies to support management and professional workers.

IMPLEMENTATION STRATEGIES

Williamsburg Clothiers

Williamsburg's management chose to set up word processing technology in a centralized office services group because this strategy appeared to be the most cost-effective means of meeting the rising volume of paperwork and at the same time providing customers and managers with high-quality output. But by the end of 1980, Wendy Kelly, manager of Office Services, found herself making her second request within a year for additional equipment and operators.

The company president was concerned that the Office Services group was now costing too much money. The efficiency that word processing technology and centralized office services was supposed to bring about was threatened as users began making more demands and creating new projects for the system.

Williamsburg found itself in a "control crisis" similar to what Nolan (1979) had frequently observed when looking at the implementation of data processing systems. As people gained some experience in using the technology they began to expand its applications beyond what was originally planned. This behavior came into conflict with the original "efficiency" objectives set by top management.

When it seemed that costs were getting "out of control," management wanted to restrict access to the technology or apply some other kind of cost-cutting techniques. There was no "push" from management to use the equipment to support managerial activity or to go beyond the immediately apparent issues of output efficiency.

After gaining some experience with the technology and expanding its applications, Williamsburg's view of word processing was still efficiency oriented. This finding was mirrored by the survey results as we shall see in the next chapter: Although respondents had upgraded the technology and expanded its range of applications, the overwhelming majority remained in an early stage of evolution and their use of the technology fell short of the full implementation defined earlier in this chapter.

At Williamsburg this implementation gap seemed to be caused by two factors. First, Williamsburg top management was skeptical about what gains could be made by increasing managerial productivity. Because the concept of restructuring work (and using the technology) to promote effectiveness was inherently loose, top managers were unwilling to commit hard dollars for such soft savings.

This attitude persisted even as Williamsburg continued to hire new MBAs at a much faster rate than clerical personnel to meet the demands of a growing business. Williamsburg management was certainly aware of the consulting reports and business articles that had been written, urging the use of office automation technology to increase managerial productivity. They were also aware of the growing managerial payroll. They were, however, unwilling to commit resources to any technology that could not show a clear payback. Indeed, it was unclear just how Williamsburg might use the technology as a way to reduce the number of managers it was hiring, or to make the ones it had more productive. The company remained unwilling to explore any of these possibilities even on a pilot basis.

Another reason that Williamsburg was reluctant to explore word processing beyond the obvious typing uses was the company's history of keeping clerical operations simple. When Williamsburg was a small family business, Mr. and Mrs. Alden did most of their own typing, or had one private secretary who helped them. In its early days the company had very few layers of personnel -- family members did almost everything from meeting customers to balancing the books.

Williamsburg's structure still reflected some of that "family" influence. The company was proud of its tradition of emphasizing simplicity in correspondence and communications. Managers answered their own phone calls, kept their own files, and talked to each other in person or on the phone rather than writing memos. Despite the clear benefits of keeping communications simple, there are measurable costs associated with having highly paid managers take the time to do jobs such as filing, which could be done by less-well-paid individuals. Nevertheless, answering the phone and maintaining files were part of the culture at Williamsburg. "We don't have a lot of administrative assistants or other clerical personnel around here, we keep things simple. Managers are not hiding behind a wall of secretaries," were sentiments frequently voiced in defense of Williamsburg's policy.

There were some managers who expressed privately that money spent on one or two support people would yield a high payback in terms of the saving in management time. This, however, was not the popularly held belief.

In the long run, Williamsburg is likely to be pushed by the technology itself into considering some management applications. Office Services and Data Processing were beginning to work together in 1980 in areas of common interest where the two groups could share expertise and support each other's objectives. Eventually merging of the technology may create a greater range of opportunities for such things as distributed data/word processing.

In the absence of a major crisis, it seemed unlikely that Williamsburg would change its outlook on the role of word processing in the corporation. This is partly a result of the reasons already discussed, but also, in fairness to Williamsburg, there is little in the management literature to suggest how a company actually ought to go about expanding its use of the technology beyond the typing capability.

Corning Glass Works

At Corning the implementation of word processing technology has been a long-term learning process. It, too, concentrated on applications where the hard dollar savings seemed to be most visible. Corning did, however, begin to incorporate the view, based on experience, that the technology could also assist in work restructuring and management delegation, which had the potential of providing even more returns to the company than an improvement in typing productivity alone could.

It is important to note that Corning management was willing to explore possibilities and to learn. Their experience taught them about some of the pitfalls as well as the possibilities associated with implementing a word processing/office automation system.

Corning learned that bringing about any meaningful change in the line divisions required the cooperation and expertise of both the Administrative Services group and the division managers. It also learned that work restructuring brought about some resistance as well as the need to reevaluate job titles, pay rates, and responsibilities. The Administrative Services group together with the line divisions had to develop ways of dealing with these issues that changes in the technology had initiated.

An innovator in the glass business, with a heavy investment in R&D, Corning has traditionally participated in a number of academic research projects, both at the technical and business levels. As a company, it seems more willing than most to study and analyze its own behavior.

The study conducted in the International Division was done by two professors from Cornell University who used Corning as a research site to learn about the impact of new technologies on organizational behavior and design. Since that time, the company has participated in other studies, including this one, aimed at learning more about office automation and implementation strategies. In addition to this, Corning belongs to two study groups, the Office Technology Research Group and the Office Automation Roundtable, whose members meet to share experiences and discuss new ideas.

This kind of research orientation probably was helpful to Corning's development of a learn-as-you-go strategy for implementation. Since Corning emphasizes the importance of strong line divisions, a staff function such as Administrative Services has to work hard at gaining the support of individual product managers. The staff group's willingness to learn, and change direction if necessary, was an important part of forming a good working relationship with the product division managers.

At Corning this was done without a strong commitment from top management. Even though Corning's 1980 payroll showed, for the first time, that white-collar workers made up more than 50 percent of the total payroll dollars, office automation was not a top corporate priority. Administrative Services had to contend with the view that office automation was simply not that important to the glass business. They have, therefore, proceeded slowly but steadily at building support among the division managers.

For a decentralized manufacturing company like Corning, this strategy probably makes the most sense. Although it has not achieved the same degree of technological integration or widespread change that Lincoln Life has, it has succeeded in bringing about an increased awareness of the technology's potential and pushed its use beyond the mere mechanization of typing tasks. There is every indication that the company will continue to proceed in this direction.

Lincoln National Life Insurance Company

Lincoln Life's approach to word processing occurred in two separate phases. In the early 1970s the company's objective was to improve productivity in text output in a central typing pool. After 1978 the company looked at word processing somewhat differently. It became tied to two important companywide programs: quality commitment and the automated office system.

The Quality Commitment program represented a radical shift in insurance company management practices. Caught in the vise of inflation and spiraling costs, top managers at Lincoln were willing to try a radical new approach to improve productivity. From their point of view, improving productivity was a matter of corporate survival. Without some dramatic change, they felt

Lincoln would be unable to make a reasonable profit in the insurance business.

After studying various plans, Lincoln adopted the Quality Commitment Program based on the premise that workers should have more responsibility and control over their own jobs. As a result of this policy, the nature of almost everybody's job was drastically changed. Clerical jobs were broadened considerably to make them more interesting. Workers in many departments were given control over how work would be divided, as well as the scheduling of vacation and personal days.

While most people were very enthusiastic about Quality Commitment, it was not without some casualties. First-line supervisors and middle managers particularly found it difficult to adjust. As one manager told the author, "Insurance companies were notorious white-collar sweat shops. The work was often fragmented and boring, and there were very strict rules about how things should be done. For example, everyone used to take a coffee break at precisely 10:00 AM — not 10:20 or 9:45 — but 10:00 AM. When workers began to schedule their own break time, some managers couldn't handle it and quit."

There was widespread agreement that the Quality Commitment program had been a major factor in the success of the automated office system. First, the Quality Commitment program had been such a radical change that a shift to new office technology seemed moderate by comparison.

The second important factor was that Quality Commitment had already begun the process of management delegation and work restructuring. In terms of implementing an automated office system, the Quality Commitment program provided a strong foundation.

The automated office system was essentially developed by a top-down planning approach. Word processing was incorporated with data processing by an edict from the senior staff committee. The data processing group had given top priority to the development of a distributed data processing system that would provide Lincoln's underwriters and other managers with quick access to computer power. With such access managers could make better decisions about the specifics of policy coverage or bids on reinsurance. From the beginning of its planning effort, Lincoln emphasized the importance of designing a multifunction terminal that could provide desk-top access to word/data processing and communications capabilities.

Top management supported Data Processing's initial investment of $500,000 for a prototype. This was an important step in the implementation process. The budget allocation for the prototype and the hiring of new personnel were clear signals that top management was serious about implementing the automated office system.

Top management then established the Automated Office System (AOS) group, which assumed responsibility for marketing the system throughout the company. It was responsible for helping various departments and planning for the system. It also provided the necessary training and technical expertise.

After an initial trial in Data Processing, the AOS group concentrated on the most receptive user groups in the organization. One of the first things the AOS group did was to provide training for executive secretaries so that they could assist their bosses in using the system. A secretary who was more knowledgeable about the technology was an impetus for managers themselves to learn.

Top management support was critical in this phase as well. Most of Lincoln's senior managers, including the president, had terminals on their desks and used them. This created a certain amount of pressure for subordinates to begin using the technology.

Thus the earliest users of the system were powerful as well as enthusiastic missionaries for AOS. By creating this core group of early adapters, management reasoned that more skeptical or reluctant users would gradually be converted. This is a classic approach to diffusing a new technology, documented by Rogers and Shoemaker (1971) and substantiated by subsequent research, including a recent study on information systems by Lee Gremillion (1979).

Part of Lincoln's success at implementing the AOS was influenced by the industry and competitive environment and partly by factors intrinsic to the company itself. First, as an insurance company it considered itself a "paper factory" and gave high priority to office automation. Unlike Corning, managing paperwork was considered a critical success factor and was important to the company's survival.

Lincoln's early purchase of the MT/ST, even before it could be cost justified, is further evidence of the company's long-term commitment to explore various solutions to the problems associated with managing a huge paperwork output. Giving top priority to managing paper and information is typical of the insurance industry as a whole. In the Information Systems 1980 survey of word processing usage by industry, insurance was ranked as the number one user of word processing systems.

Within the company itself, top management exhibited a certain boldness in decision making. Their across-the-board implementation of the Quality Commitment program and their commitment of substantial resources to the AOS prototype seem to indicate a higher-than-average willingness to take risks. Perhaps this risk profile and action orientation are a result of competing in the somewhat riskier-than-average reinsurance business where Lincoln is the market leader.

There was also probably less management resistance at Lincoln to using desk-top terminals than in other executive suites. This is because almost all top officers of the company have been trained as underwriters. While this does not mean they are computer experts, they are probably more mathematically and statistically oriented than the typical executive.

The nature of the planning and implementation process was also affected by certain aspects of the company's structure. The top-down implementation of the AOS was certainly made easier by the fact that Lincoln was a fairly centralized one-industry business with 3,500 of its employees physically located in two buildings in Fort Wayne, Indiana.

In a decentralized company like Corning, which operates in different businesses, it is unlikely that such an approach would be carried out as successfully. In terms of ongoing implementation, the establishment of the Automated Office Systems group was an important tactic. Like the Administrative Services group at Corning, AOS took responsibility for implementing the system and working with the various departments to establish and achieve productivity improvement objectives.

Another important aspect of this organization implementation was the technical support that AOS provided. As people learned to use the equipment, they often came up with suggestions for customizing the technology to make it more useful for them. For example, the system had a calendar function that many managers found convenient to use. An inquiry to the system would reveal a manager's first available date. The inquirer could then set up a tentative date for that time, subject to confirmation. While the system seemed to work fairly well, a group of managers suggested that some sort of "override" provision be made so that superiors or other senior managers could "bump" peers or subordinates and always get on the calendar.

The AOS group reviewed the suggestions with managers and worked on incorporating them into the technology. In addition to this specific kind of technical assistance, the AOS staff helped establish user groups and workshops so that technical expertise could be built up and spread throughout the organization.

In addition to technical modifications, there were organizational issues as well that use of the technology began to highlight. For example, the AOS group made take-home terminals available for managers and many began taking advantage of this option and found it helpful in getting additional work done. The question then arose as to whether nonprofessional clerical workers could also work at home using these terminals. This raised issues of compensation, liability, as well as equity.

Nonprofessional employees had not previously been paid for working at home, on a regular basis. Also, Workmen's Compensation provided coverage for accidents that occurred on the job during working hours. What if someone were injured while working at home? Would they be covered?

There was also the question of equity. Would receptionists or telephone operators, whose jobs demanded that they physically be in the office, resent people in other jobs, receiving similar pay, who could work at home? The Quality Commitment program had set up work groups in the various departments who had responsibility for addressing these questions. This meant that the company had a mechanism for evaluating new ideas that had the potential to reshape job responsibilities and basic work content. This was an important part of Lincoln's overall implementation effort, since it meant that new ideas could be evaluated fairly and, if desirable, incorporated into new ways of doing things. This kind of ongoing evaluation and work restructuring was critical to Lincoln's ability to hold staff levels constant while increasing volume over 20 percent. In terms of the traditional measure of productivity — output divided by input — Lincoln had achieved an impressive gain.

6
SURVEY DATA

This chapter will review and analyze the more quantitative data from the questionnaire survey of 21 responding companies. The analyses consist primarily of nonparametric statistical techniques specifically suited to small samples or data that involve "ranking tests" rather than purely numerical data.

Information gathered from the cases and survey data will be analyzed to determine if there are any discernible patterns of organization behavior or any insights that might be useful in developing a practical and generalizable theory of implementation for office automation technology.

The first section of the chapter describes the content of the questionnaire and participants' responses. The next five sections are organized under the headings of the five research questions dealing with whether an implementation gap was observed in this sample and whether the organizations' experience with the technology followed a pattern of evolutionary change. The final section presents the author's interpretation of the results and the conclusions. Appendix C contains the detailed findings from the questionnaire.

QUESTIONNAIRE CONTENT AND PARTICIPANTS' RESPONSES

The survey questionnaire, based on information gathered in the case studies, was sent to 30 member companies of the Office Technology Research Group. It was divided into two sections: one focused on the initial purchase and use of equipment and the other on any subsequent changes after word processing technology was introduced. The purpose of the questionnaire was to determine if organizations had evolved through the hypothetical

stages described in the literature. Responses were received from
21 companies. Their experiences were analyzed through the four
variables of the conceptual framework: purchase decision criteria, technology, portfolio of uses, and organizational structure.
(See Appendix Tables C.1–C.7 in Appendix C.)

Initial Purchase Decision Criteria

Initial purchasing decisions of the questionnaire respondents
showed many similarities to those reported at the case sites.
The median year of investment was 1972, with a range from 1966
to 1978. The highest median scores for respondents' ratings of
eight specified criteria for their initial decisions to invest were
need for faster output, need to keep up with rising volume of
paper work, and need for better-quality output. Only one company stated any additional reason: a need for better overall
productivity.

Technology and Initial Choices

The type of word processing equipment first installed again
paralleled the experience of the three case sites: 69 percent
were electronic typewriters or stand-alone nondisplay units, 22
percent were stand-alone display units, and 9 percent were
time-sharing. No respondents initiated word processing with a
clustered system or multifunction terminal.

Of the survey participants, 47 percent reported that three or
fewer vendors were considered as possible suppliers, 25 percent
had considered 4 to 10 vendors, and 22 percent more than 10.
The companies named 14 different suppliers in a list of vendors
initially chosen, although 79 percent initially chose IBM as at
least one of their vendors, while 21 percent chose Wang and 21
percent Vydec.

Criteria most important in choosing a vendor were overall
quality of service, ease of operation, and (tied) compatibility
with future systems and overall reputation for reliability. Again
the responses were consistent with data gathered from the three
case sites.

Initial Use of the Technology

Participants' responses to the question of what applications
they initially envisioned for the word processing technology were
consistent with the initial view of the technology as an "automated typewriter."

Of the respondents, 84 percent said they first used the equipment for form letters or work requiring extensive revisions; only one respondent (5 percent) indicated that initial use of the equipment was for broader correspondence or communications; 11 percent indicated it was used for some combination of word and data processing applications.

Organizational Structure

On organizational structure, 30 percent of the respondents indicated that word processing was originally in a decentralized location, reporting to a local manager, as had been the case at Williamsburg and Corning; another 25 percent (5 of 20 respondents) also indicated that it was initially decentralized but reported to an administrative or corporate manager; 20 percent (4 out of 20) said word processing was in a centralized location, reporting to an administrative or corporate manager.

The following five sections examine the issue of the implementation gap to find how changes in the capabilities of the technology or companies' experience with it affected the process of achieving successful implementation and overall productivity improvement (see Appendix Table C.8).

QUESTION 1

Is there an observable gap between system potential and actual use? Was this observed in isolated cases or regularly?

In terms of our definition of an "implementation gap," asking the question of whether we observed a "gap" between system potential and actual use is equivalent to asking whether most organizations observed were "mature" in their use of the technology. "Maturity" was measured principally by looking at whether the use of word processing had brought about any change in management jobs.

Only 3 of 21 respondents indicated that such a change had occurred (see Appendix Table C.8). The vast majority of organizations had not evolved along this critical dimension. Therefore we can conclude that an implementation gap was identified in a majority of cases.

The remaining research questions are directed at identifying the factors that could potentially contribute to closing this gap.

QUESTION 2

> To what extent does the evolution of the technology work to close the "implementation gap?" Does this evolutionary process affect how users decide to purchase and utilize the technology?

To explore any significant difference between organizations that purchase the technology at an earlier or later stage of its evolution, we can isolate the variables that seem to be affected by the evolutionary movement of the technology itself, as separate from change based on organizations' experience with it. We will focus on the initial purchase and use behavior of "early" and "late" adopters of the innovation (see Appendix Tables C.9–C.13).

The survey data contain responses from 21 companies, whose initial year of purchase ranged over a 12-year span from 1966 to 1978. In analyzing the data the author used various combinations of "break years" to categorize "early" and "late" adopters and to test for consistency of responses.

To perform the statistical analyses two nonparametric tests -- the Kruskal-Wallis analysis of variance by rank and the Mann-Whitney U test -- were applied to the survey data. Both of these tests are used to measure population differences. The Kruskal-Wallis test is useful for deciding whether some number of independent samples are from different populations. Sample values almost always differ somewhat; the question is whether these differences signify genuine population differences or whether they represent merely chance variations as would be expected from several random samples from the same population.

If in fact there is a significant difference between the responses of "early" and "late" adopters, we would expect the Kruskal-Wallis test to reveal this variability as an underlying population difference. The Mann-Whitney test is similarly used when there are two independent samples and one variable to be measured. Like the Kruskal-Wallis test it measures whether variability of response is the result of an underlying population difference.

Both the Kruskal-Wallis and the Mann-Whitney tests showed that there was not a significant difference on overall decision criteria for "early" and "late" adopters. Both groups initially invested in word processing equipment to keep up with the rising volume of paperwork and to get faster, better-quality output. Only one criterion, "need for better quality," was significantly more important to organizations that initially purchased the technology after 1975 or after 1978.

A similar pattern, showing no overall difference between early and late adopters, appeared in measuring responses of both groups on vendor criteria. Again only one criterion, "amount of operator training required," showed a significant difference between the two groups when 1978 was used as a break year. It was more important to companies whose initial purchase was made before 1978. For both groups, quality of service, ease of operation, and the vendor's overall reputation for reliability were most important.

Organization variables showed no significant difference between early and late adopters in how word processing was initially organized or where it reported. But in making the initial purchase decision, "late" adopters were more likely to involve a task force or corporate staff in the investment decision. Neither group showed a significant difference in the impact of word processing technology on management jobs.

For the technology variables of choice of equipment and initial application, a higher mean score for Group II indicated that late adopters bought more sophisticated equipment (not available to early users) and were more likely to use the equipment for a broader range of applications. Early adopters had equipment that was harder to use and stuck to form letters and work requiring revisions.

The evidence presented in this section seems to indicate that the evolution of the technology does affect some aspects of purchasing behavior. Late adopters involved corporate management in the initial investment decision, possibly as a reaction to some of the publicized incompatibility problems encountered by users who did not coordinate technical decision making. As the technology evolved, corporate management began to view word processing as more than a mere typewriter replacement. The more sophisticated equipment available to late adopters also made a difference between the two groups in the type of technology and applications they had to start with.

The data do not show, however, that late adopters are more likely to go beyond efficiency issues to use the technology in support of management activities. Their applications seem well within the bounds of Zisman's (1978) Stage I concept of mechanization. There was no evidence that late adopters were more concerned with overall productivity or that broad product lines or compatibility with future systems were significantly more important to them.

QUESTION 3

Does the use of word processing equipment follow an evolutionary pattern similar to that observed by other researchers in the area of MIS? Did experience with the technology bring about better use of the system's potential?

This section focuses on the changes that occurred as a result of an organization's experience with technology. The survey questionnaire was divided into two sections to examine differences between participants' initial purchase behavior and use of the technology and subsequent changes in behavior brought about by experience (see Appendix Tables C.14-C.23). To analyze the data the author applied a binomial test — a test of goodness of fit between the hypothesized characteristics of the population (that is, the null hypothesis) and the data itself.

In this case, we would assume that if shifts actually do occur, as in the stages model proposed by Nolan (1979) and others in the MIS field, at least one-half of the respondents within the sample population would have changed along the specific parameters of technology, purchase decision criteria, applications, and organization structure.

The test results indicate that there was no significant change between initial and subsequent purchase decision criteria. Later acquisitions of word processing equipment were apparently bought for the same reasons as initial purchases of equipment.

We found no significant shift among the companies surveyed to giving more consideration to effectiveness or overall productivity issues as they gained experience with the technology. Both initial and subsequent purchases of equipment were made primarily to improve efficiency of paper work output.

One vendor criterion, "compatibility with future systems," was more important in the respondents' subsequent decisions than in their initial ones. This probably indicates a greater awareness among experienced users of the potential of the technology and a greater concern that any new equipment provided by vendors should be easy to upgrade or integrate with other systems.

A significant number of respondents changed the location of the word processing function and where it reported in the corporation. The most interesting finding here was that the direction of the organizational change did not show a consistent pattern, but was "reactive" rather than "planned." For example, companies who initially organized word processing in a centralized configuration wanted a subsequent structure that was more decentralized. The opposite was also true. Companies who initially had a decentralized word processing group were pushing for more central control. The same phenomenon was true on the issue of where the word processing function reports in the organization.

One-half of the respondents in the survey indicated that this kind of organizational shift had occurred. Experience by itself was not enough to bring about any change in management jobs. Some new management jobs, such as "word processing administrator," reflected more widespread use of the technology, but there was no evidence that this had led to changes in other staff or line management jobs.

Organizations did significantly upgrade their technology and increase the range of applications. Again, this reflects advantages from the evolution of the technology for late starters rather than the experience of organizations over time.

In looking at the overall question of an evolutionary pattern we can summarize the results as follows: Only 3 respondents out of 21 indicated that use of the technology brought about any change in management jobs. The vast majority of organizations had not evolved along this critical dimension. Although users did broaden the number of applications done on the technology, these tasks were well within the range of correspondence or secretarial functions.

On the question of purchase decision criteria we found no evidence of evolution or change. Both initial and subsequent decisions seemed to be made for the same reasons: Cost reduction or improved typing output.

On the technology variable, we did find that experienced users had upgraded their technology and attached significantly more importance to a vendor's ability to provide equipment that could be upgraded or integrated with other systems. Experienced users did expand their range of applications, but this was due at least in part to the expanding capabilities of the technology itself and they were largely correspondence-related activities.

Organizational structure did change, but in no discernible pattern. For example, companies who initially organized word processing in a centralized configuration wanted a subsequent structure that was more decentralized. The opposite was also true. Companies who initially had a decentralized word processing group were pushing for more central control. The same phenomenon was true on the issue of where the word processing function reports in the organization. Organizations seemed to be responding to whatever limitations the initial structure had, by putting in its opposite. What the data showed was "reactive" rather than "planned" change.

Looking at the variable of how the investment decision was made, the data indicated that subsequent decisions were more likely to be made with the involvement of a task force or corporate-level committee than by one department manager. Most companies' initial investment was made by one department manager.

There is no evidence to suggest that evolution toward more successful implementation occurs in the absence of a specific strategy to increase managerial effectiveness. Use of the equipment, principally as a tool for increased typing output, persisted even as companies gained experience with the technology (seven years was the median level of experience) and upgraded their equipment. Purchasers of word processing technology do not appear simply to evolve toward greater management use of the technology based solely on experience or the increased capability of the hardware. Using the concept of "stages" developed by Nolan (1979) and Zisman (1978), and the definition of implementation success discussed earlier, we were unable to identify any significant evolution beyond Stage I for most organizations. As we saw in the Corning and Lincoln cases, use of the technology beyond the mechanization level seems to require the active intervention of management who view the technology as a catalyst for a variety of job and organizational changes that ultimately bring about the more widespread productivity gains promised by office automation technology.

QUESTION 4

Do organizations evolve from being users of word processing to use of a broader range of office automation technology?

The evidence presented in the previous two sections suggests that users do "evolve" along the technology dimension in that they buy more sophisticated equipment. Word processing, while it was used initially in most organizations as a kind of automated typewriter for handling form letters, has provided most companies with a base for other office automation technologies.

Vendors themselves are providing their customers with a much broader range of applications built into the machines. There is evidence from the survey data that users themselves have increased the number of word processing applications. This evolution to a broader range of technology and applications is also supported by the case data.

In general, the notion that word processing is the first experience, for most companies, with office automation technologies seems to be borne out by the experience of this sample of users.

QUESTION 5

Do organizations learn from their experience in data processing?

There is no evidence here to suggest that they do. Most of the initial decisions to purchase word processing equipment were made without the involvement of data processing personnel. These decisions were also made without considering the integration of the existing data processing base with the new word processing technology. Companies seemed to make some of the same mistakes that the early users of data processing had made. Even restructuring word processing into whatever configuration was the opposite of its initial structure was similar to what Nolan observed and described in his stages of evolution model. In general, there was no evidence that users were "smarter" about implementing word processing systems or that they were able to avoid some of these pitfalls based on their experience with data processing.

CONCLUSIONS

The research findings from both the case and survey data did reveal that the majority of companies in this sample (19 out of 21) fell short of "implementation success" as we have defined it. This is consistent with the observations made in the general business press that while many companies are utilizing a variety of office automation technologies, few have succeeded in making a substantial impact on managerial or professional productivity. This remained true even as companies purchased more sophisticated equipment and gained experience in using it. Without the active intervention of management pushing use of the technology beyond the typing function, companies tended to remain at a fairly narrow, mechanized level of technology use. Movement toward using word processing to achieve greater overall productivity does not appear to be "evolutionary" in the sense that it will simply occur over time. Successful implementation seems to require active management involvement in bringing about the necessary organizational and technological changes required for broad productivity improvements.

We did find evidence that improvements in the technology did have an impact on the way organizations purchased and used the equipment. This seems to reflect a greater awareness of the technology's potential to impact the corporations. Also, as the technology itself has become more sophisticated, the "typewriter replacement" view has given way to the concept of word processing as part of a broader system of office automation technology.

In this sample all the companies we observed began using word processing equipment to improve typing efficiency. This is consistent with Zisman's idea that office automation begins with a "mechanization" stage where structured repetitive tasks are performed by the equipment. This initial emphasis on mechanization is at least partly the result of the limited technological capabilities of the early word processors. The equipment first sold had little capacity to do more than improve the output of repetitive typing.

Mechanization of these structured tasks also provided a logical starting place for most companies. The output improvements could be measured fairly easily so that the investment seemed reasonable. The research findings did not show that evolution beyond this "mechanization" stage occurred as an inevitable result of experience. In the absence of a specific strategy to address the issues of managerial productivity or work restructuring, companies seemed to remain at this "mechanized" level or were pushed by the technology itself into a strategy that was largely reactive. This kind of reactionary policy usually means a painful change for the organization. This was the case at Williamsburg. As the capability of the technology increased, and the organization gained experience with it, use of the equipment was beyond original applications. This created a "control crisis" stage similar to what Nolan had observed in studying the use of data processing systems. There was no evidence from this study that organizations had learned from their experiences in data processing and thus were able to avoid some of the pitfalls that data processing users had encountered.

It may be that as the technology evolves toward multifunction terminals and execution work stations, and relatively cheap personal computers, users will be "pushed" into dealing with the issues of work restructuring and managerial productivity. In the companies we looked at, however, this has not yet occurred.

Based on what we do know from the research, we will describe in the following chapter a set of management recommendations for formulating an effective implementation strategy. We will also address the question of why companies appear to "get stuck" at this relatively low level of technology use.

7
HYPOTHESES AND RECOMMENDATIONS

One of the most persistent questions in implementation research is why, in spite of nearly 30 years of experience with electronic computing technologies and a great deal of research on managing change, is there such a high degree of uncertainty associated with implementing an office automation system?

Why, for example, were we able to observe such a range of implementation "successes" even within a fairly small sample of organizations? Why did Corning and Williamsburg differ so markedly in how they used the same basic word processing technology and in the results they were able to achieve? Finally, why was there such a widely observed gap between the potential of the technology to provide dramatic improvements in productivity, such as we saw at Lincoln, and its actual use in the majority of organizations studied?

HYPOTHESES

The seeds of an answer to these and other similar questions seem to be found in the basic nature of the technology itself. Computer-powered applications such as word processing, data processing, decision support systems, computer-aided design, computer-aided manufacturing, as well as the artificial intelligence applications of robots, can be differentiated from more traditional "industrial" technologies along the following two dimensions: type and range of the technology's application and use, and type of learning required for effective use.

The computer-based systems listed are all dedicated to the same type of applications: expanding the intellectual power of the human brain. The electronic components and the plastic box that house them look quite similar for a home computer, a word processor, or a small business data processing system. It is the way in which the machine is used that defines its application and its market. Information is the raw material or basic input to the process that each system performs.

In addition to this, the range of their use is considerably broader than for traditional "industrial" technologies. These "intellectual technologies" are flexible and malleable. A computer-based system can be manipulated in virtually unlimited ways to solve problems or organize information. The ways in which the technology is used are largely determined by the people who want the information rather than by the hardware itself. Because of this flexibility, people who use the technology are continually learning and revising the methods by which they solve problems or process information. This phenomenon was alluded to by Gorry and Scott-Morton (1971) when they suggested that over time managers would learn to restructure problems and decisions to take advantage of the technology's capability. This kind of continued and evolving learning process is not characteristic of industrial technologies where a product's use is more fully embodied within the hardware itself and its range of applications much more narrow. The range of applications for intellectual technologies is almost unlimited.

In addition to these distinctions in type and range of application there is also a difference in the type of learning required for effective use. Figure 7.1 arrays example technologies along a continuum where "industrial technologies" are shown to require mostly "Type A" learning and "intellectual technologies" are shown to require both "Type A" and "Type B" learning.

Within this context we define Type A learning as the specific training required to operate the technology. Training involves the acquisition of a predetermined set of skills that can be specified a priori and standardized. In this sense it is not necessary to have ongoing feedback between the learner and the technology; there is little uncertainty about what must be learned. It is essentially Argyris' (1970) "single loop learning." An example of Type A learning might be learning to drive a car, ride a bicycle or operate a large bulldozer. Certainly, this sort of learning can be a complex process; yet it is a finite one wherein the characteristics of proficiency can be determined and measured fairly clearly.

Type B learning, on the other hand, is an adaptive process that is ongoing and iterative. Unlike Type A learning, the dimensions and direction of the learning cannot be easily specified in advance. The task requires assessment and implementation of the potentiality of the technology rather than an effort to make the technology "work" properly. As with Argyris' "double loop learning," the learner significantly influences the decision as to what must be learned.

FIGURE 7.1
Technological Spectrum

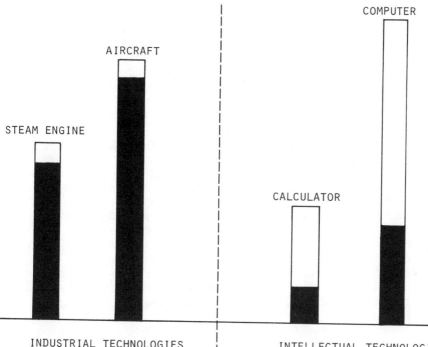

In other words, while industrial technologies often require advanced training and experience for operation, the ways in which the technology will be used or applied to perform its tasks is usually known in advance. Thus, they do not require the kind of ongoing iterative learning that characterizes intellectual technologies. It is important to note that this is different from saying that a given industrial technology may have an unknown range of applications in its early years of development. For example, the wide range of applications for electric motors may not have been obvious at their inception, but learning how to use a hair dryer, power tool, or lathe requires only Type A learning.

Intellectual technologies, on the other hand, require both Type A and Type B learning. For example, effectively using a home computer requires that the individual learn how to turn it on and off, type information into it — in short, become trained in its use. Additionally, however, the user must also learn to write programs and how to apply the technology to a variety of problem-solving activities. This may require changes in behavior (for example, savings withdrawals and deposits for later computer entry rather than writing them down as they occur), or developing whole new conceptualizations of old problems (for example, the shopping list as an inventory control problem). This sort of learning — applying the technology to a variety of problems — is an ongoing process that in fact is "customized" for the user and the set of problems to be addressed. Successful implementation means going beyond utilizing the technology to solve the obvious and structured problems, to address those situations where the outcomes cannot be specified in advance.

We saw at Corning, for example, that using word processing technology to bring about improvements in managerial productivity required reassessing the importance of some jobs, restructuring and delegating others. This was an ongoing process of learning and evaluation. The exact dimensions of the changes in job content, work procedures, or the application of the technology could not have been specified in advance; they had to be learned through experience.

This kind of "double loop" learning was typical of Lincoln's experience as well. Once people became "trained" in using the technology, they began to explore ways to use it more effectively to do their jobs. In some cases this meant programming the terminals to provide specific information, such as sales or casualty data. In other cases, "more effective use" meant restructuring work and work habits so that some jobs could be delegated while others were performed at home rather than in the office.

The major part of the productivity gains for Corning and Lincoln came about from this kind of ongoing and adaptive learning. Each company used the technology to support a wide range of work activities and procedures.

All three companies studied showed improvements in typing productivity, which was largely the result of becoming "trained" in using the technology. Williamsburg, however, was not able to go beyond this level of use because its concept of word processing was that of an automated typewriter designed only to increase secretarial output. It was unwilling to provide any of the support required for experimentation and learning that was necessary to push the use of the technology beyond the mechanization level.

The differences in "success" that were found in this sample were not a result of differences in the technology itself, but rather in the ways in which organizations used it. This widely-observed variability in how the technology was used seems to be a characteristic of what we have defined as "intellectual technologies." This variability exists because the technology itself is so flexible and its use not as narrowly confined by the hardware. Rather, the application of the technology seems to be confined by the user's imagination and ability to creatively apply the technology.

For industrial technologies, evolution can be described in terms of the evolution of product and process alone. It is not necessary to separately consider the application or use of the technology, because the product and its use are so closely tied together that they are, for practical purposes, inseparable. The evolution of each can be characterized by similar patterns, following product/process life cycle notions.

With intellectual technolgies, however, the product and its application are sufficiently separate that their evolution is driven by different forces. The application of an intellectual technology requires an ongoing learning process that is not characteristic of industrial technologies. This notion of the user's learning process is not incorporated within the product/process model. Yet it is this process of user learning that drives the evolution of a particular application.

This third dimension provides a mechanism for illustrating that while the technology itself may be at a particular stage in its evolution, users vary considerably in their ability to use the same technology to its fullest potential. The traditional concepts of "early," "transitional," and "mature" thus do not refer to points in time, as is the case with the first two dimensions, but rather to the degree of sophistication achieved by the user. Effectively utilizing intellectual technologies requires both Type A and Type B learning. Therefore, it is the user's learning curve together with that of the technology and product that paces evolution (see Figure 7.2).

This phenomenon seems to exist for a wide range of applications for computer-based systems. While the underlying technology for data and word processing systems is similar, the research indicates that experience with data processing was not useful in learning how to apply word processing technologies effectively.

FIGURE 7.2

Product/Use Evolution of Industrial and Intellectual Technologies

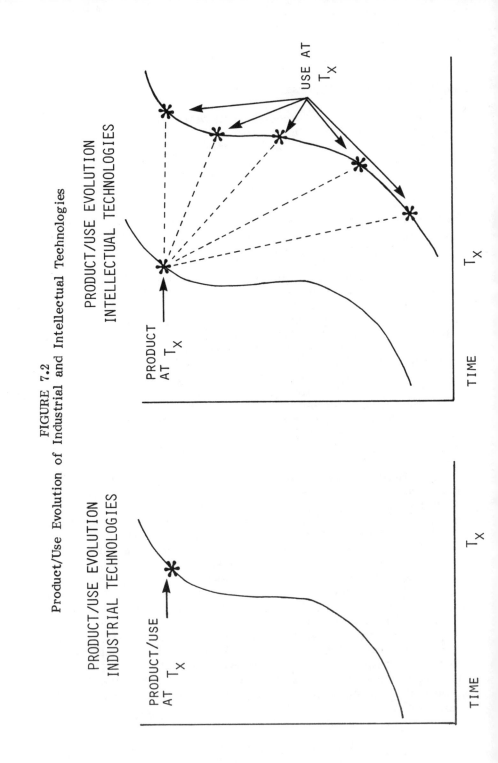

118

We would therefore suggest that each application of a computer-based system, word processing, computer-aided design, and so on, requires some level of long-term user learning to bring about full utilization of the technology's potential (see Figure 7.3).

FIGURE 7.3
Applications Life Cycle

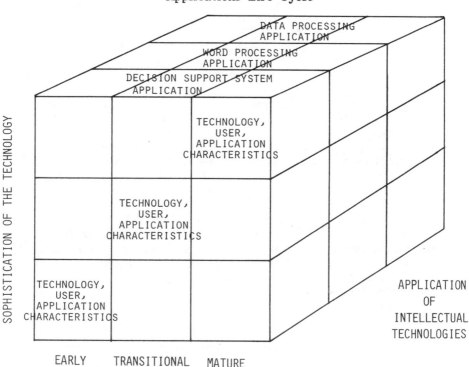

The concept of an "intellectual" technology, described by both its underlying hardware and its use, seems helpful in explaining the variety of organizational behavior observed in this study. It also provides a framework for the following recommendations to management.

RECOMMENDATIONS

Perhaps the most useful finding for managers is that organizations tend to remain at a fairly low "mechanized" level of technology utilization without an explicit strategy to do otherwise. While most companies we studied were able to show improvements in typing productivity as measured by text output per hour, or per operator, few were able to go beyond this level of use. In the survey data, only three companies indicated that the use of the technology had any impact on management jobs or the more broadly defined issues of overall white-collar productivity.

From the case studies we saw two examples — Corning and Lincoln — of companies who were able to push use of the technology beyond this level. The point of this observation is not that mechanizing typing is bad — in fact, it seems to be the logical place to start — but that remaining at this level does imply some cost or at least some foregone benefits. Applying the technology to support a broad range of office and managerial activities is important because of the competitive advantage that an increase in overall productivity is able to provide a firm.

Lincoln's 20-25 percent improvement in productivity could not have been achieved by using the technology solely as a tool to improve typing output. The competitive implications of achieving this level of productivity improvement are substantial. Lincoln now has a 25 percent cost advantage over competitors who have been unable to achieve a similar level of productivity.

Since the research findings also suggest that much of this success comes from a kind of ongoing learning and experience rather than a "plug-in" technology solution, Lincoln's head start in the learning process is probably as important as its absolute results.

Based on these research findings, the author suggests that achieving some of the much-heralded benefits of the office of the future will require the active involvement of management. Recognizing this, the following four recommendations for action are presented.

Formulate a Technology Plan

We saw from the data that both "late" adopters and experienced users recognized the need for a coordinated plan of technology purchasing. This was necessary to avoid some of the "incompatibility" problems that "early" adopters encountered. By appropriately coordinating the purchase of word processing equipment, companies were able to minimize both the technical and training incompatibilities that were often characteristic of companies where purchasing decisions were made by a variety of managers. Also, by coordinating the purchase decision, companies seemed less likely to choose "fly-by-night" vendors and were able to develop more "clout" as large customers.

A good technology plan should also address a company's future needs and whether a particular vendor can provide the necessary equipment upgrading. We saw from the survey data that experienced users were significantly more concerned than first-time users with a vendor's ability to provide equipment that was compatible with future systems.

We also saw from the data that late adopters and experienced users were more likely to involve top management or a task force of managers in the purchasing decision.

Since the technology itself is changing rapidly, it would seem appropriate to include a technical person, aware of trends in technology development, as part of the decision-making team. This becomes even more important when one considers that the various office automation technologies of data processing, word processing, and telecommunications seem to be merging together. It is important, then, for a company to recognize these trends in technological development and take them into account in the purchasing decision.

The information about available technology should then be matched with the overall information needs of the business. For this reason, a "task force" or purchasing group should comprise both general managers and technical experts who can provide the necessary guidance in formulating a purchasing plan for office automation technologies.

Recognize the Need for an Ongoing Learning Process

The potential of the technology to contribute to overall productivity beyond automating the typing function requires an ongoing learning process, the dimensions of which cannot be specified precisely in advance. We saw from the case data that Williamsburg and Corning used basically the same word processing technology in very different ways, and with very different outcomes. Corning was willing to experiment and to learn from its experience. Williamsburg, on the other hand, was unwilling to try any experimentation without a clear up-front notion of the costs and benefits involved.

As we have seen in most cases, it is simply not possible to specify in advance the exact dimensions of the changes that use of the technology will bring about. In first setting up the communications centers, Corning management had anticipated that cost savings could be realized by eliminating some secretarial positions. They found instead that secretaries were performing a range of activities that were neither useful nor meaningful to the company's business. Real cost savings eventually came about by reevaluating work, delegating tasks to the lowest-paid personnel group, and ultimately reducing the number of managers that were needed.

In formulating an implementation strategy for fully utilizing the technology's potential, managers need to be aware that such experimentation and learning is necessary and useful. This is true partly because of the nature of the technology, as we discussed in the hypothesis section, and partly because improving managerial or professional productivity is likely to be different in different businesses or industries.

For example, the way in which the technology is used to support the needs of petroleum engineers is likely to be different from the way in which a college professor or sales executive would use it. Therefore some of the more traditional capital budgeting approaches to new technology decisions seem not to apply here.

An approach to committing resources and time to learning is more typical of research and development budget outlays, yet this is precisely what a commitment to office automation is.

Williamsburg, like most other companies, did not recognize this and therefore they were unwilling to commit to the kind of experimentation necessary for major productivity improvements. This is not to suggest that managers should blindly commit unlimited resources to a vague concept of office automation, but rather that some level of uncertainty in how the equipment will be used is a characteristic of the technology and should be anticipated.

Purchasing and implementing the technology on a pilot or a trial basis probably is the preferred strategy of most organizations. Yet managers do need to be aware that even at this level of commitment the exact "payback" or nature of improvement cannot be wholly known in advance.

Be Explicit about Managing the Required Learning Process

Use of word processing or other office automation technologies requires both the Type A and Type B learning described earlier: training as well as organizational learning. The first step in managing the required learning process is to provide and encourage the necessary training. As with most new technologies, people need to gain some minimum level of competence in operating the equipment — how to turn it on and off, performing simple functions, and so on. At Lincoln, the Automated Office Systems group provided training sessions to executive secretaries even before the equipment became widely available. In addition to this, they helped establish user groups so that people could share and learn from their experiences and thus disperse technical expertise throughout the company.

This is important early in the implementation process since, as the philosophers suggest, "knowledge makes a bloody entrance." Users often get discouraged if they cannot get simple questions answered promptly. A good initial training program supported by user groups can help to provide the necessary basic skills.

Once this level of competence has been achieved, managers can then begin identifying areas where productivity improvements can be made and begin working on them. In most cases the first application for word processing is to improve typing or test output. Beyond this, managers need to encourage experimentation that is directed at using the technology to support a wide range of activities. In some cases this may mean evaluating the content of a certain job: is it necessary, are there better ways of doing it, are there other people in the organization who might be better equipped to do it? Are there ways in which the technology can be used to provide managers with greater control of their "alone" time and "group" time? Are there ways in which the technology can be used to support better-quality communications or more rapid communications?

At the same time that companies address these questions they need to establish mechanisms for evaluating what people have learned and translate that learning into changes in the technology or the organization itself.

As people begin to address questions of work restructuring or a change in job content, there needs to be a mechanism for evaluating whether the proposed changes are consistent with overall business objectives, which at the same time does not discourage people from trying new things.

We saw at Lincoln, for example, that the Quality Commitment Program had established work groups in each department that were responsible for dealing with organizational questions, such as whether secretaries could work at home. In addition to evaluating and making changes in the organizations, learning often means making some changes in the technology itself.

At Lincoln managers themselves began programming their terminals for certain key data. In addition, the Automated Office Systems group, which was located in a very visible and accessible office on the first floor, provided more advanced technical support and development.

As organizations learn, this learning should be fed back into corporate objectives and policy-setting processes. We saw at Corning that one of the initial productivity objectives, eliminating some clerical positions, had to be revised based on experience.

This refocusing of objectives is a very important part of the total learning process. We saw at Williamsburg, for example, that the objective or policy of using word processing only to lower clerical costs remained intact even as users themselves began to see new applications and potential for the technology.

When these ideas came into conflict with the original objectives, management was unwilling to evaluate these suggestions and if necessary revise their initial goals. Instead, activities that did not fall within the narrow boundaries of Williamsburg's objectives were discouraged. This prevented the kind of learning necessary to achieve overall productivity gains.

Fit Automation System into Overall Business

Planning and implementing a word processing/office automation system has to fit within the context and culture of the overall business. We saw from the case data that Corning and Lincoln used different approaches to implementing word processing/office automation technologies. Corning used a "building block" approach, where it gradually added new applications to the basic typing function of word processing. The Administrative Services Group did this by working closely with the product line managers to identify areas for improvement and set objectives for change.

This approach seems to have been an appropriate choice for Corning for two reasons:

- The product line divisions enjoy a great deal of autonomy in policy setting and operations and therefore would be unlikely to respond to a directive from a corporate staff group.
- Managing information was not seen as a critical success factor in the operation of Corning's overall business.

Top management gave office automation little attention and it is therefore unlikely that the kind of sweeping change we observed at Lincoln could have been brought about in the same manner at Corning.

At Lincoln, on the other hand, a "skeleton" approach where a sophisticated multifunction system was tried out in a series of pilot locations seems to have been the strategy with the highest payoff for them. They are a centralized, one-industry business where top management is accustomed to defining and carrying out a broad range of corporate policies. Department groups are not strong or particularly autonomous and information management was viewed as critical to the company's competitive position and ultimate survival.

The choice then of a "building block" or "skeleton" approach to implementing an office automation system seems to depend on the structure of the business and its overall planning process (Pyburn 1981) as well as the culture of the firm and the way in which it makes decisions.

Regardless of the specifics of the approach, all organizations are likely to benefit from an implementation strategy that explicitly recognizes that improvements in managerial and professional productivity require the active management of an ongoing learning process.

SUMMARY

The results of this study indicate that achievement of some of the promised benefits of office automation is not constrained by the technology, but rather by an organization's ability to use it. The challenge of office automation therefore lies with management.

As a result of this exploratory research the author has suggested a hypothesis for explaining why our ability to effectively use the technology lags behind the potential of the equipment itself. This hypothesis served as the basis for a series of management recommendations.

The challenge for future researchers would seem to be in further exploring this implementation gap and in developing a plan of office automation implementation for managers.

Appendix A
DISCUSSION AGENDA

1. Background Information on the Business
   a. Size/sales, assets
   b. Number of employees
   c. Marketing territory
   d. Growth rate
   e. Business mix
   f. Financial report information
2. The Planning Process
   a. Describe the steps involved in the original planning and implementation process for office automation technology.
   b. With the benefit of hindsight, are there any changes that you would make in the planning process?
   c. What do you think the important issue in future planning is?
3. The Business/Technology fit (Historical Perspective)
   a. What type of technology was originally purchased?
   b. What uses were originally planned?
   c. What purchase decision criteria were considered important?
   d. What vendor characteristics were important?
   e. Describe changes that have occurred over time in these areas.
4. Organizational Structure
   a. Have there been changes in organizational structure due to the use of information technology?
   b. Have there been changes in management/clerical job content?
   c. Have there been changes, in titles, or salary, since the introduction and subsequent use of the technology?

Thanks for your help.

Appendix B
QUESTIONNAIRE ON WORD PROCESSING TECHNOLOGY

The purpose of this questionnaire is to develop a profile of your company as a word processing user. The objective of this study is to better understand how word processing technology is used within your organization and what changes have occurred as the company has learned to use and assimilate the new technology.

For this reason the survey is divided into two parts: the first focusing on the initial purchase and use of the equipment, and the second focusing on the subsequent changes, if any, that have occurred since the technology was introduced.

Please complete the questionnaire as soon as possible and return it in the stamped, addressed envelope enclosed.

Thank you for your cooperation.

Kathleen F. Curley

PART I

The Initial Decision

1. Does your company presently use any word processing technology in the following 7 categories?   YES   NO
   (If YES please circle which ones are appropriate. If NO you have completed the questionnaire. Thank you.)

(1) Electronic typewriters
(2) Stand-alone nondisplay units (including MagCard, Mag Tape machines)
(3) Stand-alone single-line display ("thin window") units
(4) Stand-alone display, video screen units
(5) Clustered systems, many terminals attached to a single CPU
(6) Hybrid systems, some combination of text and data processing
(7) Time sharing

2. In what year did the company first invest in word processing equipment?

3. Please rate the importance of the following statements to your decision to invest in word processing equipment:

	Not Important			Very	Important
Need to control paperwork costs	1	2	3	4	5
Need for faster output	1	2	3	4	5
Need for better-quality output	1	2	3	4	5
Lack of qualified secretaries available	1	2	3	4	5
Need to keep up with rising volume of paper work	1	2	3	4	5
Desire to keep up with competitors using the technology	1	2	3	4	5
Desire to gain experience with office automation technology	1	2	3	4	5
Desire to better utilize secretarial time	1	2	3	4	5

4. Were there any other reasons for this decision?   YES   NO
If YES, please specify:

5. How was the decision to invest in word processing technology made? (for example, task force at corporate level, individual managers)

6. Who was involved in the decision-making process? (for example, secretaries, data processing people, consultants, top managers)

7. What initial application(s) was envisioned for the word processing technology? Please specify.

Equipment Selection

1. Approximately how many vendors were considered as possible suppliers?

2. What vendor(s) was chosen?

3. What type of equipment was first purchased?

4. What was the approximate dollar value of the investment?

5. Please rate the importance of the following vendor criteria:

	Not Important		Very Important		
Overall quality of service	1	2	3	4	5
Overall reputation for reliability	1	2	3	4	5
Delivery time	1	2	3	4	5
Low price	1	2	3	4	5
Price/performance relationship (value)	1	2	3	4	5
Vendor visibility among your top management people	1	2	3	4	5
Amount of operator training required	1	2	3	4	5
Ease of operation	1	2	3	4	5
Throughput speed	1	2	3	4	5
Compatibility with future systems	1	2	3	4	5

6. Were there any other important criteria? YES NO
   If YES, please specify:

Implementation Process

1. On a scale of 1 to 5, how would you rate the following experiences.
   (a) Generally speaking, the introduction and implementation of word processing equipment was:

1	2	3	4	5
Very Smooth				Very Difficult

(b) Generally speaking, how did the operators/secretaries react to the equipment?

1	2	3	4	5
Very Satisfied				Not Very Satisfied

(c) Generally speaking, how did managers who worked with the operators and equipment react?

1	2	3	4	5
Very Satisfied				Not Very Satisfied

2. Generally speaking, did the technology meet expectations in terms of

(a) Cost:

1	2	3	4	5
Very Satisfied				Not Very Satisfied

(b) Quality:

1	2	3	4	5
Very Satisfied				Not Very Satisfied

(c) Throughput time:

1	2	3	4	5
Very Satisfied				Not Very Satisfied

3. Was the equipment utilized as planned?   YES   NO
    If NO, please comment.

Organizational Impact

1. Were there any clerical jobs eliminated because word processing technology was introduced?

                                          YES   NO
    If YES, how many?

2. Was this result anticipated beforehand?

                                          YES   NO
    If NO, please explain.

3. What was the impact of word processing technology on:
   (a) clerical job titles?
   (b) clerical job skills?
   (c) clerical pay rates?
   (d) clerical job responsibilities?
   (e) clerical staff reporting relationship?

4. Did the introduction of word processing technology bring about any changes in management jobs?

                         YES   NO

   If YES, how?   (Please describe.)

5. Is the word processing function in your company:

         Centralized   or   Clustered/decentralized?

6. To whom does it report?

7. Looking back on your company's initial experience with word processing systems, are there any aspects of the overall process of selection, implementation, and so on, that in your opinion should have been done differently?

PART II

Subsequent Changes

   In this section we would like you to describe any changes that have occurred within your organization as a result of an increased expertise and experience with word processing technology. The idea that the application and diffusion of computer–based technologies takes place in evolutionary stages has been well documented and accepted by researchers and practitioners in the field of data processing. Our interest is in finding out if a similar evolutionary pattern is characteristic of word processing technologies. For this reason we would like you to briefly describe the changes, if any, that have taken place in the following categories since your firm's initial introduction of word processing technology.

If none has occurred, simply write "none" under each of the appropriate headings. If there has been a change please describe it as fully as possible.

1. The Technology.

   Have there been any changes in the type of equipment used? Please describe.

   Have you changed vendors?

2. Use of the Technology

   Has there been a change in the type of work that is now done on word processing equipment?

   Has there been a change in the number of people/ departments that now use the technology?

3. Purchase decision criteria.

   Has there been a change in the cost/benefit criteria used to evaluate a word processing investment?

   Has there been a change in the way you evaluate product characteristics?

   Has there been a change in the way you evaluate vendor characteristics?

4. Organizational structure.

   Have there been any changes in clerical job responsibilities, pay rates, or required skills, and so on. Please explain.

   Have there been any changes in management jobs? Please describe.

   Have there been any changes in how the word processing function is organized, to whom it reports?

5. Are there any <u>other</u> areas of change that you think are important to describe? Please explain.

Thank You!

Name_____

Company_____

Phone_____

Appendix C
QUESTIONNAIRE SURVEY DATA

APPENDIX TABLE C.1
Purchase Decision Criteria

Question: Please rate the importance of the following statements to your initial decision to invest in word processing equipment.

	1	2	3	4	5	6	7	8	9	10	11	12	13	14	15	16	17	18	19	20	21	Score Median/Rank
Need to control paper work costs.	1(a)4	1	4	5	2	2	5	2	5	3	3	3	5	5	3	1	1*	3	5	2	4	3 / 5
Need for faster output.(b)	5	5	4	4	4	4	3	5	5	5	5	5	4	5	5	5	5	4	3	5	3	4.1 / 1
Need for better quality output.(b)	3	3	5	4	4	2	3	4	4	5	5	5	4	5	2	4	5	4	4	5	2	3.7 / 3
Lack of qualified secretaries available.	1	3	1	3	1	2	3	2	3	3	3	2	3	1	2	1	2	2	2	1	2	1.7 / 8
Need to keep up with rising volume of paper work.(b)	3	5	4	5	3	4	4	5	4	5	3	3	4	5	5	3	5	4	4	2	5	3.8 / 2
Desire to keep up with competitors using the technology.	2	1	3	3	1	1	1	1	4	4	1	3	2	2	2	2	2	4	5	5	1	1.8 / 7
Desire to gain experience with office automation technology.	1	5	3	2	2	4	3	2	5	4	3	3	3	2	1	2	2	4	5	5	3	2.3 / 6
Desire to better utilize secretarial time.	4	4	5	5	4	4	4	4	4	4	4	5	4	4	3	3	5	3	1	2	5	3.5 / 4

(a)1 = not important; 5 = very important.
(b)Highest three.

Question: Were there any other reasons for this decision? Yes   1 Respondent
If yes, please specify.   Achieve greater overall productivity.

135

APPENDIX TABLE C.2
Making the Investment Decision

Question: How was the initial decision to invest in word processing technology made? By individual managers = 1; by individual managers with a task force and/or assistance from data processing = 3; by corporate staff or top management involvement = 5.

	Company Number																				
	1	2	3	4	5	6	7	8	9	10	11	12	13	14	15	16	17	18	19	20	21
Initial decision to invest	1	1	5	1	3	5	1	5	1	1	5	5	5	5	1	1	3	1	3	5	1

46.7 percent = 1.
14.2 percent = 3.
38.0 percent = 5.

APPENDIX TABLE C.3
Initial Choice of Equipment

Question: What type of equipment was originally chosen?
1 = Electronic typewriters and stand-alone non-display units (includes MagCards/MTST)
2 = Time sharing
3 = Stand-alone display units
4 = Clustered or "shared logic" systems
5 = Hybrid or multifunction systems

	Company Number																				
	1	2	3	4	5	6	7	8	9	10	11	12	13	14	15	16	17	18	19	20	21
Type of equipment	1	1	3	-	1	1	1	1	1	1	-	1	1	3	1	1	1	1	1	1	1
	2									2							3	3			

Summary statistics (should be x percent of total equipment chosen was this type):
69 percent = 1
9 percent = 2
22 percent = 3
0 = 4
0 = 5

APPENDIX TABLE C.4
Initial Vendor Selection

Question: What vendor (or vendors) was initially chosen?

Company Number	1	2	3	4	5	6	7	8	9	10
Choice of vendors	IBM (Bowne Time Share)	IBM	DEC	IBM Lexitron Vydec 3M AB Dick	—	Xerox IBM Vydec	IBM Vydec Word Plex Wang	Redactron CPT Xerox	IBM	IBM (Bowne Time Share)

Company Number	11	12	13	14	15	16	17	18	19	20	21
Choice of vendors	—	IBM	IBM	IBM Micom	IBM Lanier Redactron	Wang Micom	Wang IBM Xerox Micom NBI	Vydec	Wang IBM Xerox NBI	IBM Lanier	IBM DEC Four Phase

Summary statistics (should be read as x percent of respondents chose this company as at least one of its vendors):

79 percent = IBM
21 percent = Wang
21 percent = Vydec
16 percent = Xerox
16 percent = Micom
All other vendor companies were chosen by two respondents or less.

137

APPENDIX TABLE C.5
Criteria for Vendor Selection

Question: Please rate the importance of the following vendor criteria:

| | Company Number | | | | | | | | | | | | | | | | | | | | | Score |
	1	2	3	4	5	6	7	8	9	10	11	12	13	14	15	16	17	18	19	20	21	Median/Rank
Overall quality of service*	5	4	5	5	-	4	4	5	5	3	5	5	5	5	5	5	5	4	4	-	5	4.3 / 1
Overall reputation for reliability*	3	4	5	5	-	5	4	5	4	3	5	5	5	4	3	4	5	4	4	-	5	4 / 4
Delivery time	2	3	3	5	-	3	2	3	3	3	3	3	4	2	3	5	3	3	3	-	4	2.4 / 8
Low price	2	4	1	5	-	2	2	3	3	3	3	3	2	2	3	3	4	3	2	-	2	2.1 / 9
Price/performance relationship (value)	4	5	4	5	-	2	3	4	5	5	4	3	3	4	4	3	4	4	4	-	3	3.2 / 6
Vendor visibility among your top management people	1	3	1	2	-	1	1	1	1	3	1	2	3	2	3	1	3	2	1	-	2	1.1 / 10
Amount of operator training required	3	3	3	5	-	4	4	4	3	3	3	4	4	5	4	4	4	4	3	-	5	3.2 / 6
Ease of operation*	4	3	5	5	-	4	5	5	5	5	5	5	4	5	5	5	5	5	3	-	5	4.2 / 2
Throughput speed	5	4	3	5	-	3	3	5	3	3	5	4	4	5	4	4	5	3	3	-	4	3.3 / 5
Compatibility with future systems*	1	3	5	5	-	5	5	3	3	3	5	3	3	4	5	5	4	4	5	-	3	4 / 3

*Four highest

Question: Were there any other important criteria? If YES, please specify.

                    X

11 - Broad product line   X   2 responses

12 - Vendor provided training   1 response

APPENDIX TABLE C.6

The Application of Word Processing Technology

Question: What initial application(s) was considered for the word processing technology? Please specify. Repetitive correspondence, form letters, or work requiring extensive revisions = 1; broad range of correspondence and/or communications capability = 3; combination of word and data processing, including statistical or billing packages = 5.

	Company Number																				
	1	2	3	4	5	6	7	8	9	10	11	12	13	14	15	16	17	18	19	20	21
Initial applications	1	1	5	1	-	1	1	1	-	1	5	1	1	1	3	1	1	1	1	1	1

84 percent = 1.
5 percent = 3.
11 percent = 5.

Initial Organizational Structure

Question: (1) Was the word processing function in your company initially centralized or decentralized?
(2) To whom does it report? B = Both; C = Centralized; D = Decentralized

| | Company Number | | | | | | | | | |
	1	2	3	4	5	6	7	8	9	10
Is the word processing function centralized or decentralized?	D	D	B	D	–	D	D	D	D	B
To whom does it report?	Mgr Adm Serv	Local	Both	Local	–	Adm Mgr	Local	Adm Mgr	Local	Both

| | Company Number | | | | | | | | | |
	11	12	13	14	15	16	17	18	19	20	21
Is the word processing function centralized or decentralized?	B	C	C	B	C	D	D	D	C	D	B
To whom does it report?	Both	Corp	Adm Mgr	Adm Mgr	Adm Mgr	Off Ser Mgr	Local	Local	Off Ser Mgr	Adm	Adm Ser Mgr

Summary statistics: 30 percent = Decentralized/local manager
25 percent = Decentralized/corporate or administrative manager
20 percent = Centralized/corporate or administrative
15 percent = Both/both
10 percent = Both/corporate or administrative

APPENDIX TABLE C.8
Measure of Change between Initial and Subsequent Behavior
(H_0: P = .5 that change occurs)

	Probability Value for Binomial Test
Measure of change in management jobs	.001*

*A probability below .10 indicates that the hypothesized change along this dimension did not occur.

Measure of Difference between "Early" and "Late" Adopters
on Individual Decision Criteria
(the higher the mean rank, the greater the importance of the variable)

	Group I	Group II	Mean Rank I	Mean Rank II	Mann-Whitney "U" Statistic(a)	Signi-ficance(b)
Need to control costs	"Early" Pre-1973	"Late" Post-1973	11.85	10.23	46.50	.5372
	Pre-1975	Post-1975	10.72	11.90	35.50	.6757
	Pre-1978	Post-1978	11.11	10.00	17.00	.8049
Need for fast output	Pre-1973	Post-1973	10.10	11.82	46.00	.4755
	Pre-1975	Post-1975	10.72	11.90	35.50	.6757
	Pre-1978	Post-1978	11.11	11.00	19.00	1.00
Need for better quality	Pre-1973	Post-1973	9.75	12.14	42.50	.3545
	Pre-1975	Post-1975	9.28	16.50	12.50	.0169(b)
	Pre-1978	Post-1978	10.26	18.00	5.00	.0777(b)
Lack of qualified secretaries available	Pre-1973	Post-1973	12.80	9.36	37.00	.1782
	Pre-1975	Post-1975	12.00	7.80	24.00	.1605
	Pre-1978	Post-1978	11.03	10.75	18.50	.9493
Need to control rising volume of paper work	Pre-1973	Post-1973	10.27	10.27	47.00	.5518
	Pre-1975	Post-1975	10.60	10.60	38.00	.8615
	Pre-1978	Post-1978	7.00	7.00	11.00	.3113
Desire to keep up with com-petition	Pre-1973	Post-1973	9.45	9.45	38.00	.2157
	Pre-1975	Post-1975	8.80	8.80	29.00	.3476
	Pre-1978	Post-1978	9.50	9.50	16.00	.7101
Desire to gain experience with technology	Pre-1973	Post-1973	9.23	9.23	35.50	.1595
	Pre-1975	Post-1975	9.80	9.80	34.00	.6117
	Pre-1978	Post-1978	15.50	15.50	10.00	.2693
Need for better use of secre-tarial time	Pre-1973	Post-1973	11.00	11.00	55.00	1.00
	Pre-1975	Post-1975	14.20	14.20	24.00	.1498
	Pre-1978	Post-1978	15.00	15.00	11.00	.2961

(a)Corrected for ties.
(b)A significance level below .10 would indicate that the difference in responses between Group I and Group II was statistically significant.

APPENDIX TABLE C.10
Measure of Overall Difference between
"Early" and "Late" Adopters on Vendor Criteria

Group I	Group II	Kruskall-Wallis Chi-square(a)	Significance(b)
"Early" Adopters Pre-1973	"Late" Adopters Post-1973	1.182	.554

(a)Corrected for ties.
(b)A significance level below .10 would indicate that the difference in responses between Group I and Group II was statistically significant.

143

APPENDIX TABLE C.11
Measure of Difference between "Early" and "Late" Adopters
on Individual Vendor Criteria
(the higher the mean rank, the greater the importance of the variable)

	Group I	Group II	Mean Rank I	Mean Rank II	Mann-Whitney "U" Statistic(a)	Signi-ficance(b)
Overall quality of service	"Early" Pre-1975 Pre-1978	"Late" Post-1975 Post-1978	9.20 9.65	13.00 13.00	18.00 11.00	.1406 .3277
Overall reputation for reliability	Pre-1975 Pre-1978	Post-1975 Post-1978	9.20 9.41	13.00 15.00	18.00 7.00	.1910 .1477
Delivery time	Pre-1975 Pre-1978	Post-1975 Post-1978	10.63 10.06	7.63 9.50	20.50 16.00	.2707 .8776
Low price	Pre-1975 Pre-1978	Post-1975 Post-1978	10.27 10.38	9.00 6.75	26.00 10.50	.6692 .3563
Price/performance relationship (value)	Pre-1975 Pre-1978	Post-1975 Post-1978	9.73 9.88	11.00 11.00	26.00 15.00	.6678 .7756
Vendor visibility among your top management people	Pre-1975 Pre-1978	Post-1975 Post-1978	10.07 10.59	9.75 5.00	29.00 7.00	.9141 .1519
Amount of operator training required	Pre-1975 Pre-1978	Post-1975 Post-1978	10.13 10.71	9.50 4.00	28.00 5.00	.8275 .0824(b)
Ease of operation	Pre-1975 Pre-1978	Post-1975 Post-1978	9.07 9.59	13.50 13.50	16.00 10.00	.1029 .2787
Throughput speed	Pre-1975 Pre-1978	Post-1975 Post-1978	9.27 10.06	12.75 9.50	19.00 16.00	.2421 .8877
Compatibility with future systems	Pre-1975 Pre-1978	Post-1975 Post-1978	9.03 9.41	13.63 15.00	15.50 7.00	.1146 .1484

(a)Corrected for ties.
(b)Significance below .10 indicates that the difference in responses between Group I and Group II was statistically significant for a given "break" year and criteria.

144

APPENDIX TABLE C.12

Measure of Difference between "Early" and "Late" Adopters on Initial Organizational Variables

	Group I "Early"	Group II "Late"	Mean Rank I	Mean Rank II	Mann-Whitney "U" Statistic(a)	Significance(b)
1. Was the word processing function in your company initially centralized or decentralized? (Decentralized = 1, Both = 3, Centralized = 5)	Pre-1973	Post-1973	9.70	11.30	42.00	.5099
	Pre-1975	Post-1975	10.25	11.50	28.00	.6804
2. To whom does the word processing function report? (Local manager = 1, Both = 3, Corporate or Administrative Services = 5)	Pre-1973	Post-1973	9.95	11.05	44.50	.6403
	Pre-1975	Post-1975	11.16	7.88	21.50	.2648
3. How was the initial decision to invest made? (Individual managers = 1, individual managers with a task force or assistance from data processing = 3, Corporate staff or top management involvement = 5)	Pre-1973	Post-1973	8.55	13.23	30.50	.0591(b)
	Pre-1975	Post-1975	10.32	17.50	6.00	.0884(b)
4. Was there any change in management jobs?	Pre-1973	Post-1973	10.67	9.00	15.00	.5416
	Pre-1975	Post-1975	11.00	10.00	45.00	.5416

(a)Corrected for ties.
(b)A significance level below .10 would indicate that the difference in responses between Group I and Group II was statistically significant.

145

APPENDIX TABLE C.13

Measure of Difference between "Early" and "Late" Adopters
on Initial Technology Variables

	Group I "Early"	Group II "Late"	Mean Rank I	Mean Rank II	Mann-Whitney "U" Statistic(a)	Signi-ficance(b)
1. What type of equipment was originally chosen?						
	Pre-1973	Post-1973	7.50	14.70	6.50	.0004(b)
	Pre-1978	Post-1978	8.63	16.50	2.00	.0064(b)

1 = Electronic typewriters and stand-alone nondisplay units (includes MagCards and MTST)
2 = Time sharing
3 = Stand-alone display units
4 = Clustered or "shared logic" systems
5 = Hybrid or multifunction systems

	Group I	Group II	Mean Rank I	Mean Rank II	U	Sig.
2. What initial application was originally considered for the word processing equipment?						
	Pre-1973	Post-1973	9.00	12.00	35.00	.0679(b)
	Pre-1978	Post-1978	9.50	19.50	0.00	.0003(b)

1 = Form letters or work requiring extensive revision
3 = Broad correspondence and/or communications capability
5 = Combination of word and data processing

(a)Corrected for ties.
(b)A significance level below .10 would indicate that the difference in responses between Group I and Group II was statistically significant.

APPENDIX TABLE C.14
Changes in the Purchase Decision Criteria

Question: Has there been a change in the cost/benefit criteria used to evaluate a word processing investment?

											Company Number											
	1	2	3	4	5	6	7	8	9	10	11	12	13	14	15	16	17	18	19	20	21	
Yes				X				X		X					X							X = 24 percent
No	0	0	0		0	0	0		0		0	0	0	0		0	0	0	0	0	0	= 76 percent

All respondents

Question: If yes, what are the new criteria?
"Soft" dollar savings.
Greater managerial productivity.
Increased effectiveness.

APPENDIX TABLE C.15
Changes in Vendor Criteria

Question: Have there been any changes in the way you evaluate vendor characteristics or the importance of vendor criteria?

										Company Number												Median
	1	2	3	4	5	6	7	8	9	10	11	12	13	14	15	16	17	18	19	20	21	Score
Compatibility with future systems*	5	3	5	5	-	5	5	5	5	5	5	5	5	5	5	5	5	5	5	-	3	4.4 (1)
Broad product line*			X			X	X	X										X			X	6 respondents

*These were the only two variables that showed any change/or were mentioned by respondents as important considerations for current or future systems.

APPENDIX TABLE C.16
Measure of Change between Initial
and Subsequent Behavior within Organizations
for Purchase Decision and Vendor Criteria
$(H_o: P_1 = P_2 = .5$ that change occurs)

	Probability Value for Binomial Test
1. Measure of change between organization's initial and subsequent purchase decision criteria	.013*
2. Measure of change between organization's initial and subsequent vendor criteria "Compatibility with Future Systems"	.324

*A probability below .10 indicates that the hypothesized change along this dimension did not occur.

APPENDIX TABLE C.17
Changes in Location and Management of Word Processing

Original question: Was the word processing function in your company initially centralized or decentralized and to whom does it report?

Number of Respondents		Percent of This Group That Changed	New Configuration	
Decentralized/local	6	100	4	Decentralized/corporate
Decentralized/corporate	5	20	2	Central/corporate
Central/corporate	4	50	1	Decentralized/local
Both/both	3	33	2	Decentralized/corporate
Both/corporate	2	0	1	Decentralized/local
Total	20		10	Total

50 percent of the respondents reported changes.

148

APPENDIX TABLE C.18
Making the Investment Decision

Question: How was the initial decision to invest in word processing technology made? By individual managers = 1; by individual managers with a task force and/or assistance from data processing = 3; by corporate staff or top management involvement = 5.

	Company Number																				
	1	2	3	4	5	6	7	8	9	10	11	12	13	14	15	16	17	18	19	20	21
Initial decision to invest	1	1	5	1	3	5	1	5	1	1	5	5	5	5	1	1	3	1	3	5	1

46.7 percent = 1
14.2 percent = 3
38.0 percent = 5

Question: How were **subsequent** decisions to invest in word processing technology made?

	Company Number																				
	1	2	3	4	5	6	7	8	9	10	11	12	13	14	15	16	17	18	19	20	21
Subsequent decision to invest	3	1	5	5	3	5	5	5	5	3	5	5	5	5	3	3	3	5	3	5	5

4.76 percent = 1
33.3 percent = 3
61.8 percent = 5

149

APPENDIX TABLE C.19

Measure of Change between Initial and Subsequent
Behavior on Four Organizational Variables

	Probability Value for Binomial Test
1. Measure of change in location of word processing function (for example, centralized, decentralized, both)	.588
2. Measure of change in where the word processing function reports (local, corporate, both)	.324
3. Measure of change on how the decision to invest was made (local, task force, corporate)	.332
4. Measure of change in management jobs	.001*

*A probability below .10 indicates that the hypothesized change along this dimension did not occur.

APPENDIX TABLE C.20

The Application of Word Processing Technology

Question: What initial application(s) was considered for the word processing technology? Please specify.
Repetitive correspondence, form letters, or work requiring extensive revisions = 1; broad range of correspondence and/or communications capability = 3; combination of word and data processing, including statistical or billing packages = 5.

	Company Number																				
	1	2	3	4	5	6	7	8	9	10	11	12	13	14	15	16	17	18	19	20	21
Initial applications	1	1	5	1	-	1	1	1	1	-	1	5	1	1	1	3	1	1	1	1	1

84 percent = 1
5 percent = 3
11 percent = 5

Question: Have there been any changes in the type of work that is now done on word processing equipment?

	Company Number																				
	1	2	3	4	5	6	7	8	9	10	11	12	13	14	15	16	17	18	19	20	21
Subsequent applications	3	3	5	5	-	3	1	3	5	1	5	3	3	3	3	3	5	3	1	5	3

15 percent = 1
55 percent = 3
30 percent = 5

151

APPENDIX TABLE C.21

Initial Choice of Equipment

Question: What type of equipment was originally chosen?

1 = Electronic typewriters and stand-alone nondisplay units (includes MagCards/MTST)
2 = Time sharing
3 = Stand-alone display units
4 = Clustered or "shared logic" systems
5 = Hybrid or multifunction systems

										Company Number										
1	2	3	4	5	6	7	8	9	10	11	12	13	14	15	16	17	18	19	20	21

| Type of equipment | 1 | 1 | 3 | 1 | - | 1 | 1 | 1 | 1 | 1 | - | 1 | 1 | 3 | 1 | 1 | 3 | 1 | 1 | 1 | 1 |
| | 2 | | | | | | | | | 2 | | | | | | 3 | | 3 | | | |

Summary statistics (should be read as x percent of total equipment chosen was this type):

69 percent = 1
9 percent = 2
22 percent = 3
0 = 4
0 = 5

152

APPENDIX TABLE C.22
Changes in Choice of Equipment

Question: Have there been any changes in the type of equipment used? Please describe.
1 = Electronic typewriters and stand-alone nondisplay units (includes MagCards/MTST)
2 = Time sharing
3 = Stand-alone display units
4 = Clustered or "shared logic" systems
5 = Hybrid or multifunction systems

	Company Number																				
	1	2	3	4	5	6	7	8	9	10	11	12	13	14	15	16	17	18	19	20	21
Type of equipment	4	3	4	4	-	4	3	4	5	3	-	4	3	4	4	3	5	5	4	4	4
				5			4			4			4							5	
										5											

Summary statistics (should be read as x percent of total equipment chosen was this type):
0 = 1   21 percent = 3
0 = 2   53 percent = 4
               25 percent = 5

APPENDIX TABLE C.23
Measure of Change between Initial and Subsequent Behavior on Technology and Applications Variables

	Probability Value for Binomial Test
1. Measure of change in type of equipment used	.999
2. Measure of change in type of applications used	.961

REFERENCES

Abernathy, William J. and Utterback, James M. "Patterns of Industrial Innovation." Technology Review 80, no. 7 (June/July 1978).

Adeboye, Titus. "International Transfer of Technology: A Comparative Study of Differences in Innovative Behavior." Harvard Business School, Ph.D. dissertation, 1977.

Anderson, Thomas J. and Trotter, William R. Word Processing. New York: AMACON, 1974.

Anthony, R. N. Planning and Control Systems: A Framework for Analysis. Boston: Harvard Business School, 1965.

Apodaca, Anacleto. "Corn and Custom: Introduction of Hybrid Corn to Spanish American Farms in New Mexico." In Human Problems in Technological Change, edited by Edward H. Spier. New York: Russell Sage Foundation, 1952.

Argyris, Chris. Intervention Theory and Method. Reading, Mass.: Addison Wesley, 1970.

Beer, Michael. Organizational Change and Development: A Systems View. Santa Monica, Calif.: Goodyear Press, 1980.

Bell, Daniel. "Communications Technology for Better or Worse." Harvard Business Review, May/June 1979.

Bliven, Bruce J. The Wonderful Writing Machine. New York: Random House, 1954.

Bower, Joseph L. Managing the Resource Allocation Process. Homewood, Ill.: Richard D. Irwin, 1972.

Burns, Ton and Stalker, G. M. The Management of Innovation. London: Tavistock Publications, 1961.

Business Week, June 30, 1975.

Business Week, March 24, 1980.

Business Week, April 28, 1980.

Business Week, June 30, 1980.

Business Week, November 17, 1980.

Cale, Edward G., Jr. "Implementation Standard Computer-Based Applications Programs in Multiple Site Organizations." Harvard Business School, Ph.D. dissertation, 1979.

Carlisle, James H. "The Automated Office: Making It Productive for Tomorrow's Manager." Administrative Management, January 1981.

Chandler, Alfred D., Jr. Strategy and Structure. Cambridge, Mass.: MIT Press, 1962.

Chudson, Walter, and Wells, Louis. "Acquisition of Technology from Multinational Companies by Developing Countries," Organization for Economic Cooperation and Development Report, 1975.

Connell, John J. "Information Resource Management vs. the Office of the Future." Office Technology Research Group, Executive Newsletter, February 1981.

Current, Richard Nelson. The Typewriter and the Men Who Made It. Urbana: University of Illinois Press, 1954.

Fliegel, Frederick and Kivlin, J. E. "Differences Among Improved Farm Practices as Related to Rate of Adoption." Pennsylvania Agricultural Experiment Station, University Park, Research Bulletin No. 691, 1962.

Frost and Sullivan, Inc., (New York). "An Examination of the Word Processing Industry." 1975 Report.

Ginzberg, M. J. "A Process Approach to Management Science Implementation." Massachusetts Institute of Technology, Ph.D. dissertation, 1975.

Gorry, G. Anthony and Scott-Morton, Michael. "A Framework for Management Information Systems," Sloan Management Review, Fall 1971.

Gremillion, Lee L. "Implementing Standard Computer-Based Systems." Harvard Business School, Ph.D. dissertation, 1979.

Griliches, Zvi. "Hybrid Corn: An Exploration in the Economics of Technological Change." Econometrica 25, no. 4 (October 1957).

Hayes, Monson H., Jr. "The Psychological Barrier to Technology." Dun's Review, August 1979.

Hruschka, E. and Rheinwald, H. "The Effectiveness of Pilot Farms." Sociologica Ruralis 5 (1965):101-11.

Hunter, Dard. Papermaking: The History and Technique of an Ancient Craft. New York: Alfred A. Knopf, 1943.

Huysmans, J. H. B. M. The Implementation of Operations Research: An Approach to the Joint Consideration of Social and Technological Aspects. New York: John Wiley, 1970.

"IBM Ups the Word Processing Ante." Electronics, July 3, 1980, pp. 95-96.

Keen, Peter G. W. "Implementation Research in OR/MS and MIS: Description Versus Prescription," Stanford University Graduate School of Business, Research Paper No. 390, July 1977.

Kivlin, Joseph E. "Characteristics of Farm Practices Associated with Rate of Adoption." Pennsylvania State University, Ph.D. dissertation, 1960.

Kleinschrod, Walter A. "Word Processing: Foundation for the Office of the Eighties." New York Times, October 28, 1979.

Kolb, D. A. and Frohman, A. L. "An Organization Development Approach to Consulting." Sloan Management Review 12 no. 1 (1970):51-65.

Kotter, John. Organizational Dynamics: Diagnosis and Intervention. Reading, Mass.: Addison-Wesley, 1978.

Kotter, John; Schlesinger, Leonard A.; and Sathe, Vijay. Managing the Human Organization. Cambridge, Mass.: Harvard University Press, 1979.

Kulkowsky, Edward. "The Word Processing War Is On." Financial World, July 1-5, 1980, pp. 18-22.

Langrish, John. "Technological Determinism." In Humanizing the Workplace, edited by Richard N. Ottaway. London: Croom-Helm, 1977.

Lawrence, Paul R. and Lorsch, J. Organization and Environment. Homewood, Ill.: Richard D. Irwin, 1969.

Leavitt, H. T. et al. New Perspectives in Organizational Research. New York: John Wiley, 1964.

Lewin, K. "Group Decision and Social Change." In Readings in Social Psychology, edited by Eleanor E. Maccoby, Theodore M. Newcomb, and Eugene L. Hartley. New York: Henry Holt, 1958.

Lodahl, Thomas. "Integrated Cost Benefit Analysis." Address given at Office Automation Seminar, Sloan School of Management, Massachusetts Institute of Technology, May 6, 1980.

Lodahl, Thomas and Meyer, N. Dean. "Six Pathways to Office Automation." Administration Management, February 1980.

Lodahl, Thomas and Williams, L. K. "Organizational Software for Designing the Automated Office," National Computer Conference Paper, 1977.

Loving, Rush, Jr. "At Lanier a Better Mousetrap Isn't Quite Enough." Fortune, February 26, 1971, p. 70.

Lucas, Henry C. "The Evolution of an Information System: From Key Man to Every Person." Sloan Management Review, Winter 1978.

Mansfield, Edwin. The Economics of Technological Change. New York: W. W. Norton, 1968.

Mansfield, Edwin et al. Research and Innovation in the Modern Corporation. New York: W. W. Norton, 1971.

Markham, Jesse. "Market Structure, Business Conduct, and Innovation." American Economic Review, 77th Annual Meeting of AEA, December 28-30, 1964.

Marquis, Donald G. "The Anatomy of Successful Innovations." Innovation 7 (1969).

Microelectronics, A Scientific American Book. San Francisco: W. H. Freeman, 1977.

Miles, Robert and Kimberly, John. The Organizational Life Cycle: Issues in the Creation, Transformation, and Decline of Organizations. San Francisco: Jossey-Bass, 1980.

Miller, Frederick. "Word Processing Salary and Equipment Survey." Information Systems, June 1980, p. 56.

Mumford, Enid. "Values, Technology and Work." In Reader in Organization Sociology, Manchester Business School, England.

Nasbeth, L. and Ray, G. F. The Diffusion of New Industrial Processes. Cambridge: Cambridge University Press, 1974.

Nolan, Richard. "Managing the Crises in Data Processing." Harvard Business Review, March-April 1979.

Nolan, Richard and Gibson, Cyrus. "Managing the Four Stages of EDP Growth." Harvard Business Review, January-February 1974.

Noyce, Robert N. "Microelectronics." Scientific American 237, no.3 (September 1977):62.

Petrini, Frank. "The Rate of Adoption of Selected Agricultural Innovations." Agricultural College of Sweden (Uppsala), Report No. 53, 1966.

Porter, Michael E. Competitive Strategy: Techniques for Analyzing Industries and Competition, New York: The Free Press, 1980.

Pyburn, Philip J. "Information Systems Planning: A Contingency Perspective." Harvard Business School, Ph.D. dissertation, 1981.

Radnor, M.; Rubenstein, A. H.; and Tansik, D. A. "Implementation in Operations Research and R & D in Government and Business Organization," Operations Research 18 (1970):967-91.

Rogers, E. M. and Shoemaker, F. Diffusion of Innovations. New York: The Free Press, 1962.

Rogers, Everett M. and Shoemaker, F. Floyd. Communication of Innovations: A Cross-Cultural Approach. New York: The Free Press, 1971.

Schein, E. H. "Management Development as a Process of Influence." Industrial Management Review 2, no.2 (1961).

Scherer, Frederic M. Industrial Market Structure and Economic Performance. Chicago: Rand-McNally, 1970.

Schumpeter, Joseph. Capitalism, Socialism, and Democracy. New York: Harper and Row, 1960.

Seybold Report, October 1979.

Simon, Herbert A. The New Science of Management Decision. New York: Harper and Row, 1960.

Singh, Ram N. "Characteristics of Farm Innovations Associated with the Rate of Adoption." Ontario Agricultural Extension, Report No. 14, 1966.

Slevin, Susan M. "An Annotated Bibliography on the Implementation of Operations Research/Management Science Techniques," September 1973 (unpublished).

Strassmann, Paul A. "The Office of the Future: Information Management For A New Age." Technology Review, December/ January 1980.

Tilton, John E. International Diffusion of Technology: The Case of Semi-Conductors. Washington, D.C.: Brookings Institution, 1971.

Utterback, James M. "Innovation in Industry and the Diffusion of Technology," Science, February 14, 1974.

Vernon, Raymond. The Economic and Political Consequences of Multinational Enterprise: An Anthology. Boston: Harvard Business School, Division of Research, 1972.

VonHippel, Eric. "The Dominant Role of Users in the Scientific Instrument Innovation Process." Research Policy 4 (1976).

Wang Annual Report, 1979.

Weir, Mary. "Are Computer Systems and Humanized Work Compatible?" In Humanizing the Workplace, edited by Richard N. Ottaway. London: Croom-Helm, 1977.

Zand, D. E. and Sorensen, R. E. "Theory of Change and the Effective Use of Management Science." Administrative Science Quarterly 20 (1975).

Zisman, Michael E. "Office Automation: Revolution or Evolution?" Sloan Management Review, Spring 1978.

INDEX

ABOUT THE AUTHOR

KATHLEEN FOLEY CURLEY is an Assistant Professor of Business Administration at Northeastern University. Professor Curley holds an A.B. degree from Smith College and M.B.A. and D.B.A. degrees from Harvard University's Graduate School of Business Administration. Her research has focused on the implementation of office automation technology within organizations. She has been an advisor to the U.S. Forest Service, the Office Tech Research Group, and several other organizations.

She taught the Office Automation section of Harvard Business School's Executive Education course, "Managing the Information Resource" and has written several articles and working papers on the subject.